Life Affirmations

From Scripture

Fuel for the Flame of Faith

Shelley Quinn

3ABN BOOKS
P.O. Box 220
West Frankfort, Illinois
www.3ABN.org

Pacific Press® Publishing Association
Nampa, Idaho
Oshawa, Ontario, Canada
www.pacificpress.com

Cover Design by Kenton Rogers
Cover photo by Kenton Rogers
Inside Design by Aaron Troia

Additional copies of this book are available from two locations:
3ABN: Call 1-800-752-3226 or visit http://www.3abn.org
Adventist Book Centers: Call 1-800-765-6855
or visit http://www.adventistbookcenter.com

3ABN Books is dedicated to bringing you the best in published materials consistent with the mission of Three Angels
Broadcasting Network. Our goal is to uplift Jesus through books, audio, and video materials by our family of 3ABN
presenters. Our in-depth Bible study guides, devotionals, biographies, and lifestyle materials promote the whole person
in health and the mending of broken people. For more information, call 618-627-4651 or visit 3ABN's Web site:
http://3ABN.org

Library of Congress Cataloging-in-Publication Data

Quinn, Shelley (Shelley J.), 1949-
Life affirmations : fuel for the flame of faith / Shelley Quinn.
p. cm.
ISBN 13: 978-0-8163-2278-7 (paperback)
ISBN 10: 0-8163-2278-3
1. Christian life. I. Title.
BV4501.3.Q56 2008
248.4—dc22
2008004999

08 09 10 11 12 • 5 4 3 2 1

Contents

Chapter One
Our Common Struggle

"What's wrong with me, Lord?"

The words escaping my lips startled me. It was a familiar cry of "identity crisis" from the distant past—a question I had not had to ask in many years. I didn't need to wait for the answer. I knew. I had allowed the overwhelming concerns of life and the unceasing demands of ministry to disrupt the rhythm of my relationship with God.

It wasn't a question of my salvation. I was still alive in Christ, but I was confronting a condition of "spiritual arrhythmia"—a heart attitude toward God that was skipping several beats.

As the author of *Exalting His Word*, I immediately recognized the root of my problem—I wasn't practicing what I preached. My sudden spiritual upheaval was the result of taking God's presence for granted. For the past few months, I had abandoned my daily practice of speaking affirmations from Scripture over my life.

It's amazing. When I'm not personally confessing God's promises, my spiritual passion flickers, and the identity crisis crouching in the corner rears its ugly head—no matter how much of God's Word I have stored in my heart or how much Christian service I pursue.

Passionate devotion to the person of Jesus Christ requires passionate devotion to His Word.

Confession, they say, is good for the soul but hard on the reputation. Please don't misunderstand what I'm saying. In spite of the disruption I felt in my relationship with my Lord, I was still devoted to Him and to the work of His harvest fields. I hadn't turned my back on Him, but I had turned my face. I felt we were like a husband and wife sitting side-by-side at home, speaking sporadically about events of the day—comfortable and loving with each other, yet preoccupied and taking the other for granted. They may never sign a certificate of divorce. Still, they miss the joy of enthusiastically embracing their most beloved in heartfelt conversation.

Passionate devotion to the person of Jesus Christ requires passionate devotion to His Word. God has proven this to me by experience. I'm not speaking of some emotional high; I'm speaking of sharing intimate knowledge of the character of God, knowing your true identity in Christ, and understanding the loving plan He has for you.

Confessing and affirming His promises over your life pulls down the veil that covers your identity in Christ. When your awareness of who you are "in Christ" is elevated, your Christian walk is radically different. There is a shared oneness with Him, an unshakable confidence, and a surety in His power to fulfill His purposes for you. You know that you know He will *cause* you to be all that He has *called* you to be.

Recognizing my problem, I sat down and reread *Exalting His Word,* something I had not done for many months. It was as if I had not written the book. God ministered to me then through His teaching as much as He had the first time. Suddenly I realized how far I had fallen, and my heart lamented. When the Lord first opened the way for that book, I had written it from start to finish in just seventeen days, and it didn't require editing. In my current spiritual condition, if someone had assigned me the task of committing that teaching to writing, I doubt I could have written it at all.

> *It's easy for us to allow the competition of daily events to crowd out meaningful time with God, isn't it?*

Why am I baring my soul to you like this? I don't know who you are. Maybe you've read *Exalting His Word* and are one of the thousands who have contacted me to share how powerfully God has changed your Christian experience through the practice of life affirmations from Scripture. Perhaps you're one of the hundreds of spiritual leaders who have started a Word Warrior squadron. Or it could be that you have never heard of the book and have no idea what a life affirmation from Scripture is, but you have seen me on television and think that I don't have spiritual struggles like you do.

I'm sharing this to let you know that I do. I'm no different from you—with the exception, perhaps, that you may have yet to experience a truly intimate relationship with God or walk in the transforming power of His Word. Still, even though I have practiced this great pleasure and had the privilege of sharing this God-given teaching in a book, what we have in common is that we're both humans, and we share the same struggles.

We can all find joy in a teaching of God, walk in its path for a while, and wake up one morning to discover we have gotten off track. It's like finally getting into a good physical exercise routine. Here you are looking better, feeling better—life is good! Then something interrupts your discipline. Motivation to exercise evaporates into thin air, and those optimal health benefits you were enjoying begin to dwindle. Likewise, our spiritual condition declines when we no longer continue exercising any of God's teachings.

Swarmed by activities, plagued by interruptions, it's easy for us to allow the competition of daily events to crowd out meaningful time with God, isn't it? C'mon—am I the only one who struggles with this?

Does this sound even vaguely familiar? The alarm clock rings. You hit the floor running. Pressed for time, you say a quick prayer with a *promise* to give God your full attention later. By the end of your daily whirl of activities, you discover you have taken God's presence for granted. It was an unintentional oversight—you feel frustrated by your own lack of discipline.

Your energies are spent. There's little time left to give to the One who loves you most. So, before you fall asleep, you offer up "leftovers" to God with a *promise* to do better tomorrow. At the close of the following day, your heart is broken as you realize you have repeated the same pattern of behavior yet again.

In the land of merry-go-round promises, tomorrow never comes! It's all a matter of ordering your priorities and doing what is most important first. But for most of us, it's not that easy. Protecting your devotion to God is a constant challenge that you must meet head on.

Why we allow these self-defeating episodes to occur is a mystery to me. How easy it is to lay aside something that is best for us—and how difficult it is to return to the discipline of practicing it again. I don't have the answers to life's questions, but I know the One who does, and all we need is to go to His Word to find them. As we depend upon God to stir the importance of Scripture in our hearts, He shines the light of His Word into our darkness and shows us the way out of our confusion.

If you're one of the thousands of Word Warriors who have been waiting for this sequel to *Exalting His Word,* I apologize for its delay. I also want to encourage you to revisit the original work from time to time to keep yourself on course. I think you'll find, as I have, that rereading it will help to recalibrate your compass, keeping you turned full-faced to the Lord. One dear soul told me she read *Exalting His Word* eight times in the first year she had it, and six times in the second. I've now purposed to read it once per quarter to keep my feet on a straight path.

> We depend upon God to stir the importance of Scripture in our hearts ... and show us the way out of our confusion.

The book you now hold in your hands is the sequel to *Exalting His Word.* Whereas that book was a teaching instrument to convince you of the power of practicing life affirmations from Scripture, the focus of this book is the compiled affirmations—an instrument for daily devotions.

First, though, I'll share just a few opening thoughts with you, to encapsulate the essence of the teaching. That's easier said than done, because my natural tendency is to want to repeat the entire teaching again!

Chapter Two
The Truth Will Set You Free

You really need to know only two things: What a "life affirmation from Scripture" is and why you should invest time in this affirmation process.

A life affirmation from Scripture is acknowledging God's testimony that His Word is life to us! It is simply declaring the Scriptures over your life as an assertion of faith, a proclamation of who you are in Christ. This goes beyond claiming a promise; it becomes a confession of the "word of faith" as the Bible calls it. As you affirm His Word by speaking it over your life, your thinking lines up in agreement with God's testimony about you and all that He will accomplish in your life.

> *There is ... faith-building power in hearing your own voice say these marvelous truths of God.*

Faith comes by hearing your own living voice as you confess God's Word over your life. This process changes your "self-talk"—it helps you take your thoughts captive and make them obedient to the will of God. To capture errant thoughts, you must replace them with other thoughts.

Life affirmations from Scripture cause God's way of thinking to become your way of thinking. The transforming power of His Word renews your mind and subdues your spiritual identity crisis, putting away your confusion of who you are in Christ.

There are three foundational Scriptures for this process:

1. God assures us in **Isaiah 55:11** that His Word will not return to Him void, but will accomplish His purposes. With life affirmations from Scripture, we are returning God's Word to Him in faith that His purposes will be accomplished in our lives.
2. God also tells us in **Jeremiah 1:12** that He is watching over His Word to perform it.
3. We must always remember that **Romans 4:17** tells us that God calls things that are not yet in existence as if they already were. That's often what you and I are doing with these affirmations —we may not see the result yet, but we confess it by faith and count it done in our lives.

The process is simple. All you need is to invest time each day to speak an affirmation (or affirmations) over your life—aloud, if possible. Faith truly does come by hearing. I cannot explain why, but there is more faith-building power in hearing your own voice say these marvelous truths of God than in hearing them spoken by any other human voice.

After you have spoken the affirmation, speak each Scripture aloud—including the Scripture reference. Although you are not trying to memorize Scripture in this process, you will be amazed at how it helps to hide the Word in your heart. So many people have told me that as they have spoken these affirmations, their experience has become like mine—when the Scriptures become your testimony, the Holy Spirit will bring them back to your remembrance when needed.

Finally, pray the affirmation back to God.

The Lord once impressed upon me this simple, yet profound thought: **Time is life. How you invest your time is how you invest your life.** I can guarantee you that speaking the life affirmations from Scripture will be worth the investment of time you make. It is a life-changing practice, because it causes you to abide in God's Word.

> "If you abide in My word, you are My disciples indeed.
> And you shall know the truth, and the truth shall make you free"
> (John 8:31, 32, NKJV).

This is a conditional promise. You must first abide in the Word to be set free. The process of life affirmations from Scripture will cause you to abide in God's Word—to meditate upon it and to put it into practice. God transforms your thinking to His higher way of thinking. You will know the truth about who you are "in Christ," and the truth will free you from the baggage of your past, the pressures of today, and concerns about the future. The measure of thought and study you give to His Word will be the measure of virtue and knowledge that comes back to you.

> And He said to them, Be careful what you are hearing.
> The measure [of thought and study] you give [to the truth
> you hear] will be the measure [of virtue and knowledge]
> that comes back to you—and more [besides] will be given
> to you *who hear* (Mark 4:24, AMP).

One of the most exciting benefits of life affirmations from Scripture is that they cause your spiritual DNA to undergo a transformation. Let me explain.

It has been my great privilege to be active in full-time ministry since January of 2000. By personal appearance, I have met and ministered to thousands of people each year. Top that number off with the thousands who have contacted me because of my ministry in television, and you can appreciate that I've heard my share of people's problems.

Time is life. How you invest your time is how you invest your life.

Sin shatters life. At the very least, sin fractures life.

Shattered lives are easily recognized. Through a series of moral choices—either their own or someone else's—these people have fallen to a place where the only way out is up. It's the sin-*fractured* life that is more difficult to identify, because people are masterful at masking their problems. These are the ones stabbing Christ's heart with a sword of stubborn self-will. On the other hand, perhaps the sin of self-satisfaction is corrupting them. And they sit in church and call themselves Christians.

It doesn't have to be this way! No matter what the sin problem is, there is good news. God has a plan for our lives, and it is better than the one we're living!

Our hour of triumph over sin comes only when we understand we cannot save ourselves. We are saved by God's grace, through our faith; and the glory of our salvation belongs to Him! What we all need is our Savior, Jesus Christ—the Living Word of God.

Through the transforming power of His Word and His Spirit, He will save us from ourselves. He can even bring disenchanted "Christians" from simmering to sizzling spirituality, if we will cooperate with His divine power and loving plan.

> His divine power has given to us all things that pertain to
> life and godliness, through the knowledge of Him who called
> us by glory and virtue, by which have been given to us
> exceedingly great and precious promises, that through these
> you may be partakers of the divine nature, having escaped
> the corruption that is in the world through lust
> (2 Peter 1:3, 4, NKJV).

What is Peter telling us? He is saying that in infinite love, God has provided us with all that we need for an abundant life and a godly character. All of God's promises are ours if we are abiding in Christ. As we become partakers of His promises, we become partakers of His divine nature through the transforming power of His Word. As we become partakers of His promises, we escape the corruption that is in the world.

As we become partakers of His promises, we become partakers of His divine nature through the transforming power of His Word.

With God's purpose in our hearts, our practical application of His Word, and perseverance by the power of the Holy Spirit, we will receive the promise after we have done His will (see Hebrews 10:36). By the grace of God, we gain mastery over our sinful nature.

In the physical realm, DNA chromosomes are the genetic material that gives you your identity. DNA makes you who you are. Allow me to make a comparison to the spiritual realm.

We all have what I label as spiritual DNA—either the **D**evil's **N**ature **A**cquired or the **D**ivine **N**ature **A**cquired. God grants all humanity the opportunity to change our spiritual DNA, to become partakers of the divine nature through partaking of His promises.

Think of God's Scripture promises as His divine chromosomes. The more of His chromosomes you have abiding in you, the more you become like Him. By the transforming power of

His Word and His Spirit, you become a new creation in Christ. God has made total provision for us, and He will empower us to will and to act according to His good pleasure.

Peter continues by explaining our responsibility—

> For this very reason, make every effort to add to your faith goodness . . . knowledge . . . self-control . . . perseverance . . . godliness . . . brotherly kindness and . . . love. For if you possess these qualities in increasing measure, they will keep you from being ineffective and unproductive in your knowledge of our Lord Jesus Christ. But if anyone does not have them, he is nearsighted and blind, and has forgotten that he has been cleansed from his past sins
> (2 Peter 1:5–9, NIV).

God is passionate over you, and He wants you to be passionate over Him. He wants you to make an effort to draw near to Him so that He may fill you with His love, power, and divine nature. When the flame of God's love burns within our hearts, we are aglow with zeal, filled with a holy passion for His presence—our thoughts consumed by what concerns Him, our actions ignited by reverence and awe.

Do you want a more intimate relationship with Jesus Christ? Then make every effort to develop a more intimate relationship with His Word.

If we choose the corruption of the world over the companionship of God, we overshadow the Holy Spirit's power. His power is concealed, rather than revealed, in our lives by our choice. He will not force us to act.

Do you want a more intimate relationship with Jesus Christ? Then make every effort to develop a more intimate relationship with His Word. Superficial study deposits the Word in our mind as if scribbled in sand—the winds of strife soon sweep it away. In sharp contrast, repetitive review and confession of life affirmations from Scripture inscribes God's truth in our hearts as if etched in rock—the foundation upon which the wise build their character.

" 'Is not My word like a fire?' says the LORD" (Jeremiah 23:29, NKJV). Fire consumes dross and purifies gold. God's Word in our hearts will purify the rubbish and debris of the world that has settled there and refine our characters to make us pure gold vessels for the Lord.

Life affirmations from Scripture fuel the flame of faith. We'll stoke that fire in the next chapter.

Chapter Three
Fuel for the Flame of Faith

It was February of 1996 when the Lord first gave me *Life Affirmations From Scripture.* I was up all night writing the thoughts that flashed through my mind at lightning speed. At daybreak, I had written over a hundred affirmations. The following day I searched *Strong's Concordance* and found Scriptures to support each affirmation the Holy Spirit inspired me to record.

In my previous book, *Exalting His Word,* I wrote extensively about how the Lord brought me into this teaching, including why I believed I was impressed to write most affirmations beginning with the words "I am." Now, at the risk of being misunderstood, I would like to share two very personal stories that I previously omitted.

The night after I had matched Scriptures to all the affirmations, the Lord impressed me to look into the mirror and speak the affirmations aloud. I know this must sound strange to you—it sounded strange to me. Still, I believed it was God's direction, so I did it.

Looking myself in the eyes and speaking God's Word in affirmations that began with "I am" was awkward and uncomfortable. In fact, I felt like a hypocrite—I was not who I was claiming to be. Of course, that was God's purpose in the exercise. God was teaching me to go forward by faith in His Word, and not by my feelings. He was teaching me to call things that are not as though they already were (see Romans 4:17).

> *God was teaching me to go forward by faith in His Word, and not by my feelings.*

As I grappled with feelings of inadequacy, God finally arrested my convoluted human reasoning when I spoke this affirmation: "I am sealed for the day of redemption. God has given me eternal life, and this life is in His Son. As long as I abide in Jesus, I have assurance of my salvation" (see Ephesians 4:30; 1 John 5:11, 12).

It wasn't difficult to accept these words—in some detached manner—written on paper. After all, I had Scriptures to support the statement. But it became altogether different standing in front of the mirror, speaking these words aloud and looking into the image of my own eyes. Suddenly it was personal. The light of God's Word radiated from the recesses of my mind and into my heart. I tried to blink away the pooling tears, but soon they streamed down my face. My Christian experience had always been one of fear and trembling insecurity. Until that moment, I had never enjoyed assurance of salvation or discerned the power of grace.

Several weeks later, I was at the wedding of a dear friend. This was the first Catholic wedding I had attended, and the solemnity and beauty of the service was breathtaking.

During the reception event that followed, the bride's brother led his small daughter to the dance floor. I recognized her as the "flower girl" in the ceremony. The child looked angelic in her elegant white dress, with flowers and ribbons streaming through her flowing hair. Her father's adoration was apparent. A hush fell over the crowd as all eyes fixed on the touching scene. The father tenderly placed her small feet on top of his highly-polished shoes and tightly gripped her little hands, leading her around the dance floor—her face beaming with joy!

Perhaps you have witnessed, or even participated in, this somewhat common ritual of instruction between a parent and child. My father died in a fiery plane crash when I was six years old. I can't help but wonder if we had ever shared such a moment—moving in perfect harmony, with me feeling secure in the knowledge that I was in step with him. If we did, I cannot recall it. However, I'll never forget the day I shared such a moment with my heavenly Father!

Six months after this experience at the wedding, I was speaking affirmations aloud during my time of prayer and worship with the Lord. As I heard myself say, "I walk in step with You, Holy Spirit—not lagging behind, not running ahead of You," (see Galatians 5:25)—I was painfully aware that I was calling "things that are not as though they were" (Romans 4:17, NIV). I cried out to God to teach me to walk in His ways and to keep in perfect step with His Spirit.

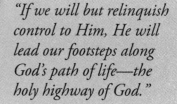

"If we will but relinquish control to Him, He will lead our footsteps along God's path of life—the holy highway of God."

Suddenly, unexpectedly, I saw in my mind two huge hands reaching down to me. I couldn't see a face or a body, just hands and feet. He placed my feet on top of His much larger feet, firmly—but tenderly—gripping my hands and leading me as we twirled around the room, rejoicing together in perfect union. I was reminded of Zephaniah 3:17—"He will rejoice over you with singing" (NKJV). (The Hebrew word for *rejoice* means to "frolic and twirl about.") Keeping in step with Him required me to relinquish total control to Him.

Then the Lord impressed this thought upon my heart. When Jesus tells us, "Follow Me," He knows He will have to do the leading. His Spirit is not somewhere across the room barking out directions, "Do it like this!" The Holy Spirit lives in us! If we will but relinquish control to Him, He will lead our footsteps along God's path of life—the holy highway of God. We can walk in Christ's footsteps if we depend completely on the Holy Spirit. He will hold fast to us and cause us to walk in perfect union with Him. As He leads us through life, it will be obvious to everyone who watches just how much our heavenly Father adores us!

> "The Lord has appeared of old to me, saying:
> 'Yes, I have loved you with an everlasting love;
> Therefore with lovingkindness I have drawn you.
> Again I will build you, and you shall be rebuilt,
> O virgin of Israel!
> You shall again be adorned with your tambourines,
> And shall go forth in the dances of those who rejoice' "
> (Jeremiah 31:3, 4, NKJV).

God is the perfect Father! He is a very personal Father, and He longs to share tender moments with His children. I have included these two stories to demonstrate how your loving Father will build your faith in His Word as you confess His Word over your life.

Without doubt, faith comes by hearing! Life affirmations from Scripture add fuel to the flame of faith.

What is faith? If you've been a Christian for long, you are no doubt answering in your mind, "Faith is the substance of things hoped for, the evidence of things not seen," (Hebrews 11:1, NKJV). That's what most Christians recite when asked to define *faith*.

But, now I have another question for you. What does Hebrews 11:1 really mean? Think about it for a moment. If you were trying to define *faith* to a non-Christian, would he or she really understand it from that one Scripture reference, or would it seem to be merely an ethereal phrase?

I believe very few people conduct their lives according to true faith, simply because they don't really comprehend what it is. How important it is that we Christians do understand. Without faith, we can't please God (see Hebrews 11:6). Why? The apostle John provides the best reason I have discovered: If we don't believe God's testimony, we are regarding Him as a liar (see 1 John 5:10). No wonder we can't please God without faith in His Word!

> *Trust in God is the foundation for faith. We've got to lean on what His Word says—and not on our own understanding.*

So what is faith? How do you grow in faith? When I speak at revival series, retreats, and camp meetings, one of my favorite teachings to include is faith. It's usually a ninety-minute session—with lots of supporting Scripture. I would like to share a quick overview of that presentation with you now, to broaden your understanding of true faith.

Let's look at seven steps to victorious faith.

1. Trust in God. Trust in God is the foundation for faith. We've got to lean on what His Word says—and not on our own understanding (see Proverbs 3:5, 6).

2. Hope. Hope is the next step up. Our hope in God's promises is the anchor for our soul that keeps us from being double-minded (see Hebrews 6:17–19). In the Greek language of the New Testament, the word *hope* means "eager expectation." As we trust in the Lord's faithfulness, knowing all of His promises are ours in Christ (see 2 Corinthians 1:20), we begin to eagerly expect Him to perform His vows.

3. Title Deed. This is the assurance, the confirmation, of the things we hope for, representing the claim we can stake on His promises. This is what gives us the evidence of things not seen. This is what allows us to perceive, by faith, His promises as real "fact" even before they have been revealed to our physical senses (see Hebrews 11:1).

4. Speaking in the spirit of faith. This is the next step. Paul defines the "spirit of faith" as believing and speaking the promises of God over our lives (see 2 Corinthians 4:13). It is the "word of faith" that is in your mouth and in your heart (see Romans 10:8). Faith comes by hearing the Word of God (see Romans 10:17).

5. Actions of obedience. This step is vital. Believing is not enough. We must *act* on our belief. Without works, faith is stillborn—it's dead (see James 2:17)!

6. A victorious attitude. A victorious attitude is critical to faith. When we're walking in faith, we have the victory that overcomes all that the world can throw at us (see 1 John 5:3, 4).

7. Standing firm. If we don't stand firm in our faith, we will not stand at all (see Isaiah 7:9). We must persevere, so that after we have done the will of God, we will receive the promise (see Hebrews 10:36).

Can you see how life affirmations from Scripture can fuel the flame of your faith? Spending time with God in His Word will increase your trust in Him. As you learn to lean on His understanding, you will find that He causes you to bubble over with hope and eager expectations of what He will do in your life. As you claim the promises, you are staking your title-deed interest in them. Then, as you speak in the spirit of faith, your faith will be bolstered as you make God's truths your testimony. You'll discover the transforming power of God's Word is at work within you, causing you to think and act differently. As you put actions of obedience into motion, you will develop a victorious attitude. The culmination of this process will be that God will help you to stand firm in faith!

Please don't forget that you are calling things that are not yet in existence as if they already were (see Romans 4:17). But, hallelujah, as you return God's Word to Him, it will not return void. It will accomplish all of His purposes (see Isaiah 55:11). You have His Word on it, and God is watching over His Word to perform it (see Jeremiah 1:12).

Paul sums it up by saying that the only thing that really counts as we live "in Christ" is faith expressing itself through love (see Galatians 5:6). Now that's a powerful statement, isn't it?

Believing in God's Word means to "be living in" God's Word. Oh, how I want you to taste and see how good the Word of God is!

> *The only thing that really counts as we live "in Christ" is faith expressing itself through love.*

The greater your knowledge of His Word, the greater your faith will be. The greater your faith, the greater your expectations will be. God wants you to increase the measure of your expectations, for with the measure you use it will be measured back to you (see Luke 6:38).

I am praying for you to make life affirmations from Scripture a part of your daily devotional life with God. I pray they will add abundant fuel to the flame of your faith. Please pray the same for me!

May the grace of our Lord Jesus Christ, the love of God, and the fellowship of the Holy Spirit be with you! May your faith be increased, and may the Lord bless you according to your faith!

Instructions: Life Affirmations From Scripture

I challenge you to set aside time each day for the next month and speak life affirmations from Scripture aloud. No matter how well you know the Scriptures—or how long you've been serving the Lord—I believe you'll find you are tapping into a spiritual power source like none other you have known before.

Here are some suggestions that I've found helpful.

1. **Devote thirty minutes** each day to this practice of meditating on God's Word. I've learned my days go much smoother when I dedicate time early in the morning. If you can't squeeze thirty minutes into your schedule in a single time slot, try dividing this practice into two fifteen-minute segments—or three ten-minute exercises.

2. **Begin with prayer.** Ask God to sanctify you by His Word (see John 17:17). Ask Him to teach you His will. Ask to be filled with His Spirit and for the Holy Spirit to be your teacher. I incorporate the speaking of affirmations into my regular prayer time. This whole practice is a process of prayer. After some rehearsal, many Christians realize a spontaneous burst of praise arises in their hearts. Most have mentioned a new level of intimacy they experience in their prayer time through this process.

3. **Speak the affirmation and supporting Scriptures aloud.** As you speak the affirmation (the words within the box), you're returning God's Word to Him. When I speak the supporting Scriptures aloud, I sense I'm hearing the voice of God. Scripture is His Word.

4. **Repeat the affirmation** after saying the Scriptures. Change the wording, if necessary, to offer direct thanksgiving to God.

5. **Conclude with prayer and praise.** Thank God for watching over His Word to perform it. Thank Him for making known "the end from the beginning." Most of all, thank Him that He calls things that are not as though they already were.

1. Abba—My Perfect Father

I am in covenant relationship with my Heavenly Father. The Lord God Almighty is my **"ABBA"** Father. He is the perfect Father—overflowing with love, slow to anger, always ready to forgive when I confess my sins, completely faithful and trustworthy. For my own good, He disciplines me for a time to correct my path. He is the Giver of all good gifts.

Genesis 17:7, NIV

"I will establish my covenant as an everlasting covenant between me and you and your descendants after you . . . to be your God."

Jeremiah 31:3, NKJV

The LORD has appeared of old to me, saying: "Yes, I have loved you with an everlasting love; Therefore with lovingkindness I have drawn you."

Galatians 4:6, AMP

And because you [really] are [His] sons, God has sent the [Holy] Spirit of His Son into our hearts, crying, Abba . . . Father!

Exodus 34:5-7, NIV

Then the LORD...proclaimed his name, the LORD. And he passed in front of Moses, proclaiming, "The LORD, the LORD, the compassionate and gracious God, slow to anger, abounding in love and faithfulness, maintaining love to thousands, and forgiving wickedness, rebellion and sin. Yet he does not leave the guilty unpunished."

1 John 1:9, NKJV

If we confess our sins, He is faithful and just to forgive us our sins and to cleanse us from all unrighteousness.

Hebrews 12:10,11, NIV

God disciplines us for our good, that we may share in his holiness. No discipline seems pleasant at the time, but painful. Later on, however, it produces a harvest of righteousness and peace for those who have been trained by it.

James 1:17, NIV

Every good and perfect gift is from above, coming down from the Father of the heavenly lights.

2. Abide in Christ and Bear Abundant Fruit

I abide (remain) in Jesus and He remains in me. I know I must continue to follow His plan and obey His commandments to remain in Him. By His grace, I do not consciously and continually sin. By the power of His vital force in me, I bear fruit. I owe Him my life. Because I bear His name, my conduct should be like Christ's.

I stay in His Word and He—the Living Word—stays in me. Therefore, I may ask what I wish that is in agreement with His will, and it will be done for me.

John 8:31, 32, NKJV

"If you abide in My word, you are My disciples indeed. And you shall know the truth, and the truth shall make you free."

1 John 3:24, AMP

All who keep His commandments . . . abide in Him, and He in them. [They let Christ be a home to them and they are the home of Christ.]

1 John 3:6, AMP

No one who abides in Him [who lives and remains in communion with and in obedience to Him—deliberately, knowingly, and habitually] commits (practices) sin. No one who [habitually] sins has either seen or known Him [recognized, perceived, or understood Him, or has had an experiential acquaintance with Him].

John 15:4, 5, AMP

Dwell in Me, and I will dwell in you. [Live in Me, and I will live in you.] Just as no branch can bear fruit of itself without abiding in (being vitally united to) the vine, neither can you bear fruit unless you abide in Me. I am the Vine; you are the branches. Whoever lives in Me and I in him bears much (abundant) fruit. However, apart from Me [cut off from vital union with Me] you can do nothing.

1 John 2:6, AMP

Whoever says he abides in Him ought [as a personal debt] to walk *and* conduct himself in the same way in which He walked and conducted Himself.

John 15:7, AMP

If you live in Me [abide vitally united to Me] and My words remain in you and continue to live in your hearts, ask whatever you will, and it shall be done for you.

3. Abiding in God's Word

God's Word is my spiritual nutrition; I live by every word that comes from His mouth. Jesus Christ sustains me by His mighty word of power. He washes away the influence of the world by the cleansing power of His Word.

The "sword of the Spirit" is the Scriptures I have hidden in my heart, daily applying them to my life. As I draw out a Scripture, I can fend off the enemy and—by God's power—cut the cord of the wicked influences that try to bind my mind.

I abide in Christ, by abiding in His Word. His words live in my heart. As I return the Word to Him in prayer, it increases the effectiveness of my prayer because my will is in perfect alignment with His will. God watches over His word to perform it. Every word of God is power-filled and possible of fulfillment. I am blessed because I believe in what the Lord has promised. Oh Lord, let it be done to me according to Your Word!

Matthew 4:4, NKJV

But He answered and said, "It is written, 'Man shall not live by bread alone, but by every word that proceeds from the mouth of God.' "

Hebrews 1:3, AMP

He is the sole expression of the glory of God [the Light-being, the out-raying or radiance of the divine], and He is the perfect imprint and very image of [God's] nature, upholding and maintaining and guiding and propelling the universe by His mighty word of power.

Ephesians 5:25–27, NKJV

Christ also loved the church and gave Himself for her, that He might sanctify and cleanse her with the washing of water by the word, that He might present it to Himself a glorious church, not having spot or wrinkle or any such thing, but that it should be holy and without blemish.

Ephesians 6:17, NIV

Take . . . the sword of the Spirit, which is the word of God.

Psalm 129:4, NIV

The LORD is righteous; he has cut me free from the cords of the wicked.

John 15:7, AMP

If you live in Me [abide vitally united to Me] and My words remain in you and continue to live in your hearts, ask whatever you will, and it shall be done for you.

Jeremiah 1:12, NASB

Then the LORD said to me, "You have seen well, for I am watching over My word to perform it."

Luke 1:37, AMP

With God nothing is ever impossible and no word from God shall be without power or impossible of fulfillment.

Luke 1:45, NASB

"Blessed is she who believed that there would be a fulfillment of what had been spoken to her by the Lord."

Luke 1:38, NKJV

"Let it be to me according to your word."

4. Above All Treasures

Jesus is the living Word, by whom all things were created. He is full of grace and truth. I desire a more intimate relationship with Him, and to accomplish this I must have a more intimate relationship with the written Word of God.

Oh Lord, give me a humble spirit! Cause me to tremble at Your Word and revere Your commands. I worship You, Lord. I praise You for Your love, truth, and faithfulness. Cause me to exalt Your Word above all else! Cause my heart to stand in awe of Your Word. Cause me to treasure it above all treasures.

Your words were found, and I ate them, and they were food for my soul! How sweet are Your words to me; they bring life! Sanctify me by Your Word—set me apart for holiness. Your Word is able to make me wise for salvation through faith in Christ Jesus. Correct me and instruct me in righteousness through Your Word that I may be complete, thoroughly equipped for every good work.

John 1:1, 3, 14, NKJV

In the beginning was the Word, and the Word was with God, and the Word was God. . . . All things were made through Him, and without Him nothing was made that was made. . . . And the Word became flesh and dwelt among us, and we beheld His glory, the glory as of the only begotten of the Father, full of grace and truth.

Isaiah 66:2, AMP

All these things My hand has made, and so all these things have come into being [by and for Me], says the Lord. But this is the man to whom I will look and have regard: he who is humble and of a broken or wounded spirit, and who trembles at My word and reveres My commands.

Psalm 138:2, AMP

I will worship toward Your holy temple and praise Your name for Your loving-kindness and for Your truth and faithfulness; for You have exalted above all else Your name and Your word and You have magnified Your word above all Your name!

Psalm 119:161, 162, NKJV

My heart stands in awe of Your word. I rejoice at Your word as one who finds great treasure.

Job 23:12, AMP

I have not gone back from the commandment of His lips; I have esteemed and treasured the words of His mouth more than my necessary food.

Ezekiel 2:8, NKJV

"You, son of man, hear what I say to you. Do not be rebellious like that rebellious house; open your mouth and eat what I give you."

Jeremiah 15:16, NKJV

Your words were found, and I ate them, and Your word was to me the joy and rejoicing of my heart; for I am called by Your name, O LORD God of hosts.

Psalm 119:103, NASB

How sweet are Your words to my taste! Yes, sweeter than honey to my mouth!

John 6:63, NKJV

"It is the Spirit who gives life; the flesh profits nothing. The words that I speak to you are spirit, and they are life."

John 17:17, NKJV

"Sanctify them by Your truth. Your word is truth."

2 Timothy 3:15–17, NKJV

You have known the Holy Scriptures, which are able to make you wise for salvation through faith which is in Christ Jesus. All Scripture is given by inspiration of God, and is profitable for doctrine, for reproof, for correction, for instruction in righteousness, that the man of God may be complete, thoroughly equipped for every good work.

5. Affirmations From Scripture Develop Faith Actions

God's Word illuminates my pathway, revealing His plan for my life—making known the end from the beginning. His Word is not idle; it is life to me!

Speaking the Word lets me hear it with my living voice (and faith comes by hearing). My spoken affirmation develops "faith actions" as I let His Word do a work within me. I am "chosen" to act—to be obedient to Christ, through the sanctifying power of the Holy Spirit and of the Word of God.

Mediating on His Word is the most valuable investment of my time. **Time is life! How I invest my time, is how I invest my life!**

Psalm 119:105, NKJV

Your word is a lamp to my feet and a light to my path.

Isaiah 46:10, NIV

"I make known the end from the beginning, from ancient times, what is still to come."

Deuteronomy 32:46, 47, NIV

"They are not just idle words for you—**they are your life.**"

Romans 10:10, 17, NKJV

With the heart one believes to righteousness, and with the mouth **confession is made to salvation.** . . . So then faith comes by hearing, and hearing by the word of God.

James 2:17, NIV

In the same way, faith by itself, if it is not accompanied by action, is dead.

1 Peter 1:2, AMP

Who were chosen and foreknown by God the Father and consecrated (sanctified, made holy) by the Spirit to be obedient to Jesus Christ.

John 17:17, NKJV

"Sanctify them by Your truth. Your Word is truth."

Psalm 19:14, NIV

May the words of my mouth and the meditation of my heart be pleasing in your sight, O Lord, my Rock and my Redeemer.

6. All God's Promises Are Mine in Christ

I let His Word dwell in me richly, that I might possess His knowledge and wisdom. I want the mind of Christ operating through me. I trust God to watch over His Word to perform it. I am confident that Almighty God has the power to accomplish everything He has promised.

All of God's promises are mine through Christ Jesus and my obedience to Him.

I regard and call God's promises that are not yet physically apparent as if they were already brought into existence.

Colossians 3:16, NKJV

Let the word of Christ dwell in you richly in all wisdom, teaching and admonishing one another.

1 Corinthians 1:30, NKJV

Of Him you are in Christ Jesus, who became for us wisdom from God.

1 Corinthians 2:16, NKJV

"Who has known the mind of the LORD that he may instruct Him?" But we have the mind of Christ.

1 Kings 8:24, NKJV

"You have kept what You promised. . . . You have both spoken with Your mouth and fulfilled it with Your hand."

Romans 4:20, 21, NKJV

He did not waver at the promise of God through unbelief, but was strengthened in faith, giving glory to God, and being fully convinced that what He had promised He was also able to perform.

2 Corinthians 1:20, NIV

No matter how many promises God has made, they are "Yes" in Christ. And so through him the "Amen" is spoken by us to the glory of God.

Romans 4:17, NKJV

God, who gives life to the dead and calls those things which do not exist as though they did;

7. All Things Are Possible Through Christ's Strength

All things are possible with God. **I can do all things through Christ Jesus**, who keeps on strengthening me with His sufficiency and power, through His Spirit in my innermost being. The power of His Holy Presence is working in me, and He will perfect His strength in me to overcome my weaknesses.

My flesh counts for nothing! Only His Spirit brings real life!

Matthew 19:26, NKJV

Jesus looked at them and said to them, "With men this is impossible, but with God all things are possible."

Philippians 4:13, NKJV

I can do all things through Christ who strengthens me.

Ephesians 3:16, NIV

I pray that out of his glorious riches **he may strengthen you with power** through his Spirit in your inner being.

Colossians 1:11, AMP

[We pray] that you may be invigorated and strengthened with **all power** according to the might of His glory, [to exercise] every kind of endurance and patience . . . with joy.

2 Corinthians 12:9, NIV

"My grace is sufficient for you, for my power is made perfect in weakness."

Galations 3:3, NKJV

Are you so foolish? Having begun in the Spirit, are you now being made perfect by the flesh?

John 6:63, AMP

It is the Spirit Who gives life [He is the Life-giver]; the flesh conveys no benefit whatever [there is no profit in it]. The words (truths) that I have been speaking to you are spirit and life.

8. Angels Watching Over Me

Ministering angels sent by the Lord surround me. Because I am abiding in Him, God commands His angels concerning me. These angels, who excel in strength, have access to my heavenly Father. They record my praise, thanksgiving, and meditation upon God in a book of remembrance. Angels watch over me for protection. With great attention, they also watch to see if my life demonstrates appreciation for the love of God and cooperation with His plan of salvation. There are more with me than my eye can see!

Hebrews 1:14, AMP

Are not the angels all ministering spirits (servants) sent out in the service [of God for the assistance] of those who are to inherit salvation?

Psalm 91:9–11, NIV

If you make the Most High your dwelling . . . then no harm will befall you, no disaster will come near your tent. For **he will command his angels concerning you** to guard you in all your ways.

Hebrews 13:2, NIV

Do not forget to entertain strangers, for by so doing some people have entertained angels without knowing it.

Matthew 18:10, NASB

"See that you do not despise one of these little ones, for I say to you that their angels in heaven continually see the face of My Father who is in heaven."

1 Peter 1:12, NIV

Things that have now been told you by those who have preached the gospel to you by the Holy Spirit sent from heaven. Even angels long to look into these things.

2 Kings 6:16, 17, NASB

He answered , "Do not fear, for those who are with us are more than those who are with them." Then Elisha prayed and said, "O Lord, I pray, open his eyes that he may see." And the Lord opened the servant's eyes and he saw; and behold, the mountain was full of horses and chariots of fire all around Elisha.

9. Anointed and Established

I am established in Christ. When I was born again, God claimed me as His child and stamped me with His seal of approval. He did this by anointing me with the Holy Spirit as a pledge (much like applying a signature to a real estate contract and offering "earnest money").

The anointing of the Holy Spirit abides in me. He teaches me all truth. God's Word is spiritual and spiritually discerned. True understanding comes as I walk in obedience, keeping in step with the Holy Spirit.

I know I am a child of God, because the Spirit of God leads me. The greater my obedience, the greater supply of the Spirit I receive from our Lord. His Spirit is the strengthening power at work within my inner being.

2 Corinthians 1:21, 22, NKJV

He who establishes us with you in Christ and has anointed us is God, who also has sealed us and given us the Spirit in our hearts as a guarantee.

1 John 2:27, NASB

As for you, the anointing which you received from Him abides in you . . . and is true and is not a lie, and just as it has taught you, you abide in Him.

1 Corinthians 2:14, NIV

The man without the Spirit does not accept the things that come from the Spirit of God, for they are foolishness to him, and he cannot understand them, because they are spiritually discerned.

Galatians 5:25, NASB

If we live by the Spirit, let us also walk by the Spirit.

Romans 8:14, NKJV

As many as are led by the Spirit of God, these are sons of God.

Acts 5:32, NKJV

"We are His witnesses to these things, and so also is the Holy Spirit whom God has given to those who obey Him."

Ephesians 3:16, NASB

That He would grant you, according to the riches of His glory, to be strengthened with power through His Spirit in the inner man.

10. An Appointed Time for God's Promises

God's Word is a treasure to me that becomes rich as I practice what it says. His word is in my heart and in my mouth. As I confess His promises over my life with my living voice, my faith is increased in the hearing. Like God, I speak of things that He foretold and promised as though they already exist, even though I have yet to see the evidence. All of God's promises are mine "in Christ."

I am returning His word to Him, and it will not return void, but will accomplish His purposes in my life. I mix the message I hear with faith so that I can receive the benefit. His promises are for an appointed time. He will hasten to fulfill them. Though the answer tarries, I wait patiently, earnestly expecting Him to watch over His word to perform it. The vision will not be behindhand on its appointed day.

Romans 10:8–10, 17, NASB

What does it say? "THE WORD IS NEAR YOU, in your mouth and in your heart"— that is, the word of faith which we are preaching, that if you confess with your mouth Jesus as Lord, and believe in your heart that God raised Him from the dead, you will be saved; for with the heart a person believes, resulting in righteousness, and with the mouth he confesses, resulting in salvation. . . . So faith comes from hearing, and hearing by the word of Christ.

Romans 4:17, AMP

God . . . Who gives life to the dead and speaks of the nonexistent things that [He has foretold and promised] as if they [already] existed.

2 Corinthians 1:20, NIV

No matter how many promises God has made, they are "Yes" in Christ. And so through him the "Amen" is spoken by us to the glory of God.

Isaiah 55:11, AMP

So shall My word be that goes forth out of My mouth: it shall not return to Me void [without producing any effect, useless], but it shall accomplish that which I please and purpose, and it shall prosper in the thing for which I sent it.

Hebrews 4:2, AMP

For indeed we have had the glad tidings [Gospel of God] proclaimed to us just as truly as they [the Israelites of old did when the good news of deliverance from bondage came to them]; but the message they heard did not benefit them, because it was not mixed with faith (with the leaning of the entire personality on God in absolute trust and confidence in His power, wisdom, and goodness) by those who heard it.

Habakkuk 2:2, 3, AMP

The Lord answered me and said, Write the vision and engrave it so plainly upon tablets that everyone who passes may [be able to] read [it easily and quickly] as he hastens by. For the vision is yet for an appointed time and it hastens to the end [fulfillment]; it will not deceive or disappoint. Though it tarry, wait [earnestly] for it, because it will surely come; it will not be behindhand on its appointed day.

Jeremiah 1:12, NASB

Then the LORD said to me, "You have seen well, for I am watching over My word to perform it."

11. Assurance of Hope—It Is Written

I am sure of what I hope for, and certain the things I do not yet see will happen. **"IT IS WRITTEN,"** and God watches to assure His Word is fulfilled.

Trust is the foundation for my hope and faith. I trust God completely and put my hope in His Word, eagerly anticipating the fulfillment of His promises in my life.

Nothing can sway me from the truth—my soul is well anchored. I live by faith, which is my "title deed" to God's promises. My faith is made operative by my actions of obedience.

Obedience is the pathway to God's blessings. When I do His will, I receive the promise.

Hebrews 11:1, AMP

Faith is the assurance (the confirmation, the title deed) of the things [we] hope for, being the proof of things [we] do not see and the conviction of their reality [faith perceiving as real fact what is not revealed to the senses].

Jeremiah 1:12, AMP

The Lord said to me, You have seen well, for I am alert and active, watching over My word to perform it.

Habakkuk 2:2, 3, AMP

The LORD answered me and said, Write the vision and engrave it so plainly upon tablets that everyone who passes may [be able to] read [it easily and quickly] as he hastens by. For the vision is yet for an appointed time and it hastens to the end [fulfillment]; it will not deceive or disappoint. Though it tarry, wait [earnestly] for it, because it will surely come; it will not be behindhand on its appointed day.

Hebrews 6:18, 19, NIV

We who have fled to take hold of the hope offered to us may be greatly encouraged. We have this hope as an anchor for the soul, firm and secure.

James 2:17, AMP

Faith, if it does not have works (deeds and actions of obedience to back it up), by itself is destitute of power (inoperative, dead).

Hebrews 10:36, NIV

When you have done the will of God, you will receive what he has promised.

12. Assurance of Salvation

I abide in Christ, keeping His commandments. I know He abides in me by His Spirit. Therefore, I have assurance of salvation. God has given me eternal life, found only in His Son. No one can snatch me from His hand. The Lord preserves me from evil, making me complete in Him. I am saved by grace, through faith—being fully persuaded that God is able to keep me by His power.

1 John 3:24, NKJV

He who keeps His commandments abides in Him, and He in him. And by this we know that He abides in us, by the Spirit whom He has given us.

1 John 5:11–13, NKJV

This is the testimony: that God has given us eternal life, and this life is in His Son. He who has the Son has life; he who does not have the Son of God does not have life. These things I have written to you who believe in the name of the Son of God, that you may know that you have eternal life.

John 10:28, 29, NKJV

"I give them eternal life, and they shall never perish; neither shall anyone snatch them out of My hand. My Father, who has given them to Me, is greater than all; and no one is able to snatch them out of My Father's hand."

Psalm 121:7, NKJV

The LORD shall preserve you from all evil; He shall preserve your soul.

Hebrews 13:20, 21, NKJV

May the God of peace who brought up our Lord Jesus from the dead, . . . through the blood of the everlasting covenant, make you complete in every good work to do His will, working in you what is well pleasing in His sight, through Jesus Christ.

Ephesians 2:8, 9, NKJV

For by grace you have been saved through faith, and that not of yourselves; it is the gift of God, not of works, lest anyone should boast.

2 Timothy 1:12, NKJV

For this reason I also suffer these things; nevertheless I am not ashamed, for I know whom I have believed and am persuaded that He is able to keep what I have committed to Him until that Day.

13. Author and Finisher of My Faith

I fix my eyes in a steady gaze on Jesus Christ, Who is my faith source. He is working in me to perfect my faith. As I consider His life and the hostility He endured, I am encouraged to go forward in faith.

Because I obey the Word of God, the presence of the Godhead lives within me. To look to Christ for faith does not require that I look afar off—He is in me! His life lived out within me is my only hope of glory (my only hope of attaining His character).

According to His power, which works mightily within me, I will be taught in all wisdom and presented complete in Christ. Through my faith, I am kept by the power of God to inherit His salvation that will be revealed in the last of time.

Hebrews 12:2, 3, NKJV

Looking unto Jesus, the author and finisher of our faith, who for the joy that was set before Him endured the cross, despising the shame, and has sat down at the right hand of the throne of God. For consider Him who endured such hostility from sinners against Himself, lest you become weary and discouraged in your souls.

John 1:1, 14, AMP

In the beginning [before all time] was the Word (Christ), and the Word was with God, and the Word was God Himself. And the Word (Christ) became flesh (human, incarnate) and tabernacled (fixed His tent of flesh, lived awhile) among us; and we [actually] saw His glory (His honor, His majesty).

John 14:23, NKJV

Jesus answered and said to him, "If anyone loves Me, he will keep My word; and My Father will love him, and We will come to him and make Our home with him."

Colossians 1:27–29, NASB

The riches of the glory of this mystery among the Gentiles, which is Christ in you, the hope of glory. We proclaim Him, admonishing every man and teaching every man with all wisdom, so that we may present every man complete in Christ. For this purpose also I labor, striving according to His power, which mightily works within me.

1 Peter 1:5, NKJV

Who are kept by the power of God through faith for salvation ready to be revealed in the last time.

14. Baptized With the Holy Spirit

Jesus baptized me into a union and communion with the Holy Spirit. I have been anointed with this awe-inspiring gift from above. The Holy Spirit teaches me God's truths and works in me to sanctify me for obedience to Jesus Christ. By His Spirit, I am given power to be delivered from sin and to be Christ's faithful witness.

John 1:32, 33, NKJV

John bore witness, saying, . . . " 'This is He who baptizes with the Holy Spirit.' "

Acts 2:38, 39, NKJV

Peter said to them, "Repent, and let every one of you be baptized in the name of Jesus Christ for the remission of sins; and you shall receive the gift of the Holy Spirit. For the promise is to you and to your children, and to all who are afar off, as many as the Lord our God will call."

Acts 11:15–17, NASB

"As I began to speak, the Holy Spirit fell upon them just as He did upon us at the beginning. And I remembered the word of the Lord, how He used to say, 'John baptized with water, but **you will be baptized with the Holy Spirit.'** Therefore if God gave to them the same gift as He gave to us also after believing in the Lord Jesus Christ, who was I that I could stand in God's way?"

2 Corinthians 1:21, 22, NIV

It is God who makes both us and you stand firm in Christ. **He anointed us,** set his seal of ownership on us, and put his Spirit in our hearts as a deposit, guaranteeing what is to come.

1 John 2:27, NASB

As for you, the anointing which you received from Him abides in you, and you have no need for anyone to teach you; but as His anointing teaches you about all things, and is true and is not a lie, and just as it has taught you, you abide in Him.

1 Peter 1:2, AMP

Who were chosen *and* foreknown by God the Father and consecrated (sanctified, made holy) by the Spirit to be obedient to Jesus Christ (the Messiah).

Acts 1:5, 8, NIV

You will be baptized with the Holy Spirit . . . You will receive power when the Holy Spirit comes on you; and you will be my witnesses . . . to the ends of the earth.

15. The Battle Belongs to God

When something or someone opposes the good plan God has for my life, I realize my struggle is not against "flesh and blood," but against spiritual forces of evil operating within the world system. I take my stand without fear—the battle is the Lord's, and He will give me the victory.

God is my very present help in times of trouble. I put my hope in His Word, knowing through Him I will push back the enemy. I have trust and confidence in God's power and authority over all situations.

Ephesians 6:12, 13, NIV

> **Our struggle is not against flesh and blood,** but against the rulers, against the authorities, against the powers of this dark world and against the spiritual forces of evil in the heavenly realms. Therefore put on the full armor of God, so that when the day of evil comes, you may be able to stand your ground.

2 Chronicles 20:15, 17, NKJV

> Thus says the LORD to you: "Do not be afraid nor dismayed because of this great multitude, for the battle is not yours, but God's. . . . You will not need to fight in this battle. Position yourselves, stand still and see the salvation of the LORD, who is with you."

Exodus 14:14, NKJV

> "The LORD will fight for you, and you shall hold your peace."

Psalm 46:1, NASB

> God is our refuge and strength, a very present help in trouble.

Psalm 119:114, AMP

> You are my hiding place and my shield; I hope in Your word.

Psalm 44:5–8, NIV

> Through you we push back our enemies; through your name we trample our foes . . . You give us victory over our enemies . . . In God we make our boast all day long.

Nahum 1:7, NKJV

> The LORD is good, a stronghold in the day of trouble; and He knows those who trust in Him.

16. Beholding and Becoming—I Become What I Behold

I am beholding the Lamb of God, focusing on His love, life, light, and power!

I become what I behold (I develop character traits of the One Who occupies my attention). I will focus on His strengths rather than my weaknesses!

I dwell on things that are honorable, pure and worthy of praise, and put into practice the things God has taught me through His Word and by example of His true servants. The God of peace is with me!

John 1:29, NKJV

"Behold! The Lamb of God who takes away the sin of the world!"

Hebrews 12:2, NIV

Let us fix our eyes on Jesus, the author and perfecter of our faith.

Psalm 17:15, KJV

As for me, I will behold thy face in righteousness: I shall be satisfied, when I awake, with thy likeness.

2 Corinthians 12:9, 10, NIV

He said to me, "My grace is sufficient for you, **for my power is made perfect in weakness."** Therefore I will boast all the more gladly about my weaknesses, so that Christ's power may rest on me. . . . For when I am weak, then I am strong.

Philippians 4:8, 9, NASB

Finally, brethren, whatever is true, whatever is honorable, whatever is right, whatever is pure, whatever is lovely, whatever is of good repute, if there is any excellence and if anything worthy of praise, dwell on these things. The things you have learned and received and heard and seen in me, practice these things, and the God of peace will be with you.

17. Blameless Before God

Through God's grace given to me by Christ Jesus, I am enriched in every way as I eagerly await His return. In faithfulness, He will strengthen me to the very end so that I may stand blameless—free from sin and guilt—in the day of our Lord Jesus Christ.

The Lord pours His love into my heart by the power of His Holy Spirit, causing me to increase in love. He causes me to be all that He has called me to be—equipping me with everything I need to carry out His will and working in me to accomplish what is well pleasing to Him. In this way, He establishes me in holiness, keeping me blameless before God at His Second Coming.

1 Corinthians 1:4–9, NKJV

I thank my God always concerning you for the grace of God which was given to you by Christ Jesus, that you were enriched in everything by Him . . . , even as the testimony of Christ was confirmed in you, so that you come short in no gift, eagerly waiting for the revelation of our Lord Jesus Christ, who will also confirm you to the end, that you may be blameless in the day of our Lord Jesus Christ. God is faithful, by whom you were called into the fellowship of His Son, Jesus Christ our Lord.

1 Thessalonians 3:12, 13, NASB

May the Lord cause you to increase and abound in love for one another, and for all people, just as we also do for you; so that He may establish your hearts without blame in holiness before our God and Father at the coming of our Lord Jesus with all His saints.

Hebrews 13:20, 21, NKJV

Now may the God of peace who brought up our Lord Jesus from the dead, that great Shepherd of the sheep, through the blood of the everlasting covenant, make you complete in every good work to do His will, working in you what is well pleasing in His sight, through Jesus Christ, to whom be glory forever and ever. Amen.

Philippians 2:13, NIV

It is God who works in you to will and to act according to his good purpose.

1 Thessalonians 5:23, 24, NKJV

May the God of peace Himself sanctify you completely; and may your whole spirit, soul, and body be preserved blameless at the coming of our Lord Jesus Christ. He who calls you is faithful, who also will do it.

18. Blessed Hope—I

I trust in God's mercy. My heart rejoices in His salvation. In this present age, God's grace has taught me to deny ungodliness and worldly lusts, to live self-controlled and in His righteous way—looking for the blessed hope of the glorious second coming of Christ!

He redeemed me and made me His own special child, eager to do His good will. I am justified by faith in Him, through Whom I gained access to this grace in which I now stand. I rejoice in hope (eager expectation) of God revealing His glory to me and in me.

Psalm 13:5, NKJV

I have trusted in Your mercy; my heart shall rejoice in Your salvation.

Titus 2:11–14, NKJV

The grace of God that brings salvation has appeared to all men, teaching us that, denying ungodliness and worldly lusts, we should live soberly, righteously, and godly in the present age, looking for the blessed hope and glorious appearing of our great God and Savior Jesus Christ, who gave Himself for us, that He might redeem us from every lawless deed and purify for Himself His own special people, zealous for good works.

Romans 5:1, 2, NKJV

Having been justified by faith, we have peace with God through our Lord Jesus Christ, through whom also we have access by faith into this grace in which we stand, and rejoice in hope of the glory of God.

19. Blessed Hope—II

I have blessed hope. I rejoice that He enrolled my name in His book of life. My hope—my eager expectation—is to experience what He has laid up for me in heaven. I walk in the truth of the grace of God—serving God acceptably, with reverence and godly fear, for my God is a consuming fire.

My heart's desire is to awake in His likeness and see His face in righteousness. I don't yet understand what I will be in my resurrected and glorified state, but I know that I will be like Him, and that is my blessed hope. When He is revealed, I will finally see Him in His glory.

Maranatha—Come, O Lord! I can't wait to see You face to face and gaze upon Your glory!

Luke 10:20, AMP

Rejoice that your names are enrolled in heaven.

Colossians 1:5, 6, NKJV

Because of the hope which is laid up for you in heaven, of which you heard before in the word of the truth of the gospel, which has come to you, as it has also in all the world, and is bringing forth fruit, as it is also among you since the day you heard and knew the grace of God in truth.

Hebrews 12:28, 29, NKJV

Since we are receiving a kingdom which cannot be shaken, let us have grace, by which we may serve God acceptably with reverence and godly fear. For our God is a consuming fire.

Psalm 17:15, NKJV

As for me, I will see Your face in righteousness; I shall be satisfied when I awake in Your likeness.

1 John 3:2, NKJV

Beloved, now we are children of God; and it has not yet been revealed what we shall be, but we know that when He is revealed, we shall be like Him, for we shall see Him as He is.

20. Blessed Hope—III

When the New Jerusalem comes down to the new re-created earth, God will dwell with us—as He originally planned at Creation. He will make all things new. Never again will I suffer the pain of death, sorrow, or crying. He will satisfy my thirsty soul with the fountain of the water of eternal life. I will be His forever.

Joy upon joy! God will reunite me with my loved ones who have fallen asleep in Christ, and I will have eternity to spend with those for whom my heart aches now. If I am alive at His coming, I will not precede into His presence without them. For at the coming of the Lord, He will shout His command, and the dead in Christ will rise first. Then we will all be caught up together to meet the Lord in the air, and thus we shall always be with the Lord!

Revelation 21:1–7, NKJV

I saw a new heaven and a new earth, for the first heaven and the first earth had passed away. . . . Then I, John, saw the holy city, New Jerusalem, coming down out of heaven from God. . . . And I heard a loud voice from heaven saying, "Behold, the tabernacle of God is with men, and He will dwell with them, and they shall be His people. God Himself will be with them and be their God. And God will wipe away every tear from their eyes; there shall be no more death, nor sorrow, nor crying. There shall be no more pain, for the former things have passed away." Then He who sat on the throne said, "Behold, I make all things new." And He said to me, "Write, for these words are true and faithful." And He said to me, . . . "I will give of the fountain of the water of life freely to him who thirsts. He who overcomes shall inherit all things, and I will be his God and he shall be My son."

1 Thessalonians 4:13–17, NKJV

I do not want you to be ignorant, brethren, concerning those who have fallen asleep, lest you sorrow as others who have no hope. For if we believe that Jesus died and rose again, even so God will bring with Him those who sleep in Jesus. For this we say to you by the word of the Lord, that we who are alive and remain until the coming of the Lord will by no means precede those who are asleep. For the Lord Himself will descend from heaven with a shout, with the voice of an archangel, and with the trumpet of God. And the dead in Christ will rise first. Then we who are alive and remain shall be caught up together with them in the clouds to meet the Lord in the air. And thus we shall always be with the Lord.

21. Blessed Hope—IV

In that great day when God destroys death and takes away all traces of my tears, I will look upon Him with wonder and say, "You are my God. I have waited eagerly for Your appearing. Thank You, Lord, for keeping me from stumbling. Because of Your love and power, I stand blameless and with great joy in the presence of Your glory. To You be honor and majesty, dominion and authority, forever and ever. Amen!"

An inheritance is reserved for me in heaven. I am kept by the power of God for eternal salvation.

As I wait expectantly for this blessed hope, the God of hope fills me to overflowing with joy and peace in believing, and causes me to bubble over with hope by the power of the Holy Spirit.

Isaiah 25:8, 9, NKJV

He will swallow up death forever, And the Lord GOD will wipe away tears from all faces; the rebuke of His people He will take away from all the earth; For the LORD has spoken. And it will be said in that day: "Behold, this is our God; we have waited for Him, and He will save us. This is the LORD; we have waited for Him; we will be glad and rejoice in His salvation."

Jude 24, 25, NASB

Now to Him who is able to keep you from stumbling, and to make you stand in the presence of His glory blameless with great joy, to the only God our Savior, through Jesus Christ our Lord, be glory, majesty, dominion and authority, before all time and now and forever. Amen.

1 Peter 1:3–5, NASB

Blessed be the God and Father of our Lord Jesus Christ, who according to His great mercy has caused us to be born again to a living hope through the resurrection of Jesus Christ from the dead, to obtain an inheritance which is imperishable and undefiled and will not fade away, reserved in heaven for you, who are protected by the power of God through faith for a salvation ready to be revealed in the last time.

Romans 15:13, NKJV

May the God of hope fill you with all joy and peace in believing, that you may abound in hope by the power of the Holy Spirit.

22. Born Again

I am born of the Spirit of God. I received Jesus Christ as my Savior and became a child of God! God's nature living within me keeps me from the continual practice of sin. He conforms my thoughts and actions to do His will. Because I am born again, I practice righteousness—God's right way of thinking and acting. Since I am born again, God empowers me to love others beyond my natural ability.

John 3:6, 7, NKJV

"That which is born of the flesh is flesh, and that which is born of the Spirit is spirit. Do not marvel that I said to you, 'You must be born again.' "

John 1:12, 13, NKJV

As many as received Him, to them He gave the right to become children of God, to those who believe in His name: who were born, not of blood, nor of the will of the flesh, nor of the will of man, but of God.

1 John 5:1, NASB

Whoever believes that Jesus is the Christ is born of God, and whoever loves the Father loves the child born of Him.

1 John 5:18, AMP

We know [absolutely] that anyone born of God does not [deliberately and knowingly] practice committing sin, but the One Who was begotten of God carefully watches over *and* protects him [Christ's divine presence within him preserves him against the evil], and the wicked one does not lay hold (get a grip) on him or touch [him].

1 John 2:29, NKJV

If you know that He is righteous, you know that everyone who practices righteousness is born of Him.

1 John 4:7, NIV

Dear friends, let us love one another, for love comes from God. Everyone who loves has been born of God and knows God.

23. Called Out of Darkness

God has opened my eyes and turned me from darkness to light—from the power of Satan to Him—that I may receive forgiveness of sins and an inheritance among those who are sanctified by faith in Christ.

He has removed the veil from my mind and heart that I might behold His glory in His holy Word—the Bible—which mirrors His image and reveals who I am "in Christ." I reflect His glory as the Holy Spirit transforms me from one level of His character to the next (progressing from glory to glory).

I am a member of a chosen generation, a royal priesthood, a holy nation that is to be an instrument of righteousness for God. He called me out of the darkness of this world system into the marvelous light of His kingdom. The brilliance of His light is so great it is unapproachable, but He causes His light to shine on me, and I am to reflect His likeness. In the midst of a crooked and perverse generation, I am shining brightly as I hold fast His Word of life.

Acts 26:17, 18, NKJV

" 'I now send you, to open their eyes, in order to turn them from darkness to light, and from the power of Satan to God, that they may receive forgiveness of sins and an inheritance among those who are sanctified by faith in Me.' "

2 Corinthians 3:18, NKJV

We all, with unveiled face, beholding as in a mirror the glory of the Lord, are being transformed into the same image from glory to glory, just as by the Spirit of the Lord.

1 Peter 2:9, NASB

You are **a chosen race, a royal priesthood, a holy nation, a people for God's own possession,** so that you may proclaim the excellencies of Him who has called you out of darkness into His marvelous light.

1 Timothy 6:15, 16, NIV

God, the blessed and only Ruler, the King of kings and Lord of lords, who alone is immortal and who lives in unapproachable light, whom no one has seen or can see.

Philippians 2:15, 16, NKJV

That you may become blameless and harmless, children of God without fault in the midst of a crooked and perverse generation, among whom you shine as lights in the world, holding fast the word of life.

24. Carry Your Cross Daily

I take up my cross daily in deliberate determination to crucify my old "sin nature." By the power of the Holy Spirit, I put to death my old way of life and bury it.

I clothe myself with Christ that I might live a resurrected lifestyle. My earnest prayer to be **continually filled** with the Holy Spirit is granted by God. I am learning to live in the power of Christ's resurrection, by the divine nature of Christ living in me.

Luke 9:23, NKJV

He said to them all, "If anyone desires to come after Me, let him deny himself, and take up his cross daily, and follow Me."

Romans 8:13, NKJV

By the Spirit you put to death the deeds of the body, you will live.

Romans 6:4–6, NKJV

We were buried with Him through baptism into death, that just as Christ was raised from the dead by the glory of the Father, **even so we also should walk in newness of life.** For if we have been united together in the likeness of His death, certainly we also shall be in the likeness of His resurrection, knowing this, that our old man was crucified with Him, that the body of sin might be done away with, that we should no longer be slaves of sin.

Romans 13:14, NKJV

Put on the Lord Jesus Christ, and make no provision for the flesh, to fulfill its lusts.

Ephesians 5:18, AMP

Ever be filled and stimulated with the [Holy] Spirit.

Philippians 3:10, 11, NIV

I want to **know Christ** and the **power of His resurrection** and the fellowship of sharing in his sufferings, becoming like him in his death, and so, somehow, to attain to the resurrection from the dead.

Colossians 1:27, NKJV

To them God willed to make known . . . the riches of the glory of this mystery . . . which is Christ in you, the hope of glory.

25. Casting Off Condemnation

When the enemy comes against me with guilt and condemnation, I pull out my sword and say—**It is written!** I am a new creation in Christ Jesus. God is working in me to cause me to will and to act according to His good pleasure. He will complete the good work He has begun in me.

My ears are open to Your Word, Lord. Trusting and relying on You, I now possess eternal life. I will not come under condemnation, but I will put on immortality at the last trumpet and be raised incorruptible. The law of the Spirit of life in me has cut me free from the law of sin and death that ruled over my old carnal nature. Because I am in Christ and walk according to the Spirit, there is now no condemnation for me.

2 Corinthians 5:17, NKJV

If anyone is in Christ, he is a new creation; old things have passed away; behold, all things have become new.

Philippians 2:13, NKJV

It is God who works in you both to will and to do for His good pleasure.

Philippians 1:6, NKJV

Being confident of this very thing, that He who has begun a good work in you will complete it until the day of Jesus Christ.

John 5:24, NKJV

"He who hears My word and believes in Him who sent Me has everlasting life, and shall not come into judgment, but has passed from death into life."

1 Corinthians 15:52, 53, NKJV

In a moment, in the twinkling of an eye, at the last trumpet. For the trumpet will sound, and the dead will be raised incorruptible, and we shall be changed. For this corruptible must put on incorruption, and this mortal must put on immortality.

Romans 8:1, 2, NKJV

There is therefore now no condemnation to those who are in Christ Jesus, who do not walk according to the flesh, but according to the Spirit. For the law of the Spirit of life in Christ Jesus has made me free from the law of sin and death.

26. Child of God

Through my faith in Jesus Christ as my Savior, I became a child of God. What manner of love this is that God has bestowed on me!

I know I am His child because I practice righteousness—His right way of thinking and acting. I walk in His light, separating myself from evil. With open arms, God receives me. He causes me to be blameless and to shine as a bright star in this dark world.

I know I am His child, because I am led by the Holy Spirit. The Spirit Himself bears witness that I am God's child. I have received the Spirit of adoption, by whom I cry out to God, "Abba (Papa), Father!"

John 1:12, NASB

As many as received Him, to them He gave the right to become children of God.

1 John 3:1, NKJV

Behold what manner of love the Father has bestowed on us, that we should be called children of God!

1 John 3:10, NASB

By this the children of God and the children of the devil are obvious: anyone who does not practice righteousness is not of God, nor the one who does not love his brother.

Ephesians 5:6–8, NKJV

Let no one deceive you with empty words, for because of these things the wrath of God comes upon the sons of disobedience. Therefore do not be partakers with them. For you were once darkness, but now you are light in the Lord. Walk as children of light.

2 Corinthians 6:17, 18, NKJV

"Come out from among them and be separate, says the Lord. Do not touch what is unclean, and I will receive you." "I will be a Father to you, and you shall be My sons and daughters, says the LORD Almighty."

Romans 8:14–16, NKJV

As many as are led by the Spirit of God, these are sons of God. For you did not receive the spirit of bondage again to fear, but you received the Spirit of adoption by whom we cry out, "Abba, Father." The Spirit Himself bears witness with our spirit that we are children of God.

27. Children—Saved by the Lord

My children enjoy great peace, because the Lord teaches them. My children are obedient to God and honor their mother and father. I will restrain my voice from weeping and my eyes from tears. My work in child rearing will be rewarded; if my children are carried away, they will return from the land of the enemy. The Lord is a righteous God, and He will save my children, cutting them free from any wickedness that may try to bind them. He will open their eyes, turn them from darkness to light—from the power of Satan to God—and give them an inheritance among those who are sanctified by faith in Christ. God will contend with the devil to save my children.

Isaiah 54:13, NKJV

All your children shall be taught by the LORD, and great shall be the peace of your children.

Proverbs 22:6, NKJV

Train up a child in the way he should go, and when he is old he will not depart from it.

Ephesians 6:2, 3, AMP

Honor . . . your father and your mother—this is the first commandment with a promise—that all may be well with you and that you may live long life on the earth.

Jeremiah 31:16, 17, AMP

Thus says the Lord: Restrain your voice from weeping and your eyes from tears, for your work shall be rewarded, says the Lord; and [**your children**] **shall return from the enemy's land.** And there is hope for your future, says the Lord; your children shall come back.

Psalm 129:4, NKJV

The LORD is righteous; He has cut in pieces the cords of the wicked.

Acts 26:18, NKJV

"To open their eyes and turn them from darkness to light, and from the power of Satan to God, that they may receive forgiveness of sins and an inheritance among those who are sanctified by faith in Me."

Isaiah 49:25, NKJV

Thus says the LORD . . . "For I will contend with him who contends with you, and I will save your children."

28. Christ's Intercession for Me

I am depending upon Christ, who lives to make constant intercession for me. He is able to save me completely and forever, as I draw near to God through Him.

I am aware of the devil's devious ways, intended to separate me from my loving Lord. When the time of testing comes and Satan tries to separate me from the Lord—like chaff from wheat—I know that Christ has already prayed for me that my faith will not fail. He watches over me day and night. He will not allow my foot to slip.

Hebrews 7:25, AMP

He is able also to save to the uttermost (completely, perfectly, finally, and for all time and eternity) those who come to God through Him, since He is always living to make petition to God and intercede with Him and intervene for them.

2 Corinthians 2:11, NASB

So that no advantage would be taken of us by Satan, for we are not ignorant of his schemes.

Luke 22:31, 32, NKJV

The Lord said, "Simon, Simon! Indeed, Satan has asked for you, that he may sift you as wheat. But I have prayed for you, that your faith should not fail; and when you have returned to Me, strengthen your brethren."

Psalm 121:3, NIV

He will not let your foot slip—he who watches over you will not slumber.

29. Comfort Overflowing

God comforts me in all my troubles. He surrounds me with songs of deliverance. **Through Christ, my comfort overflows.** I am hidden with Christ in God. He has called me by my name—I am His! He heals my broken heart. He cups His hand under my chin and lifts my head. He holds me in His everlasting arms.

2 Corinthians 1:3, 4, NIV

Praise be to the God and Father of our Lord Jesus Christ, the Father of compassion and the God of all comfort, **who comforts us in all our troubles.**

Psalm 32:7, NKJV

You are my hiding place; You shall preserve me from trouble; You shall surround me with songs of deliverance.

Colossians 3:3, AMP

For [as far as this world is concerned] you have died, and your [new, real] life is hidden with Christ in God.

Isaiah 43:1–3, AMP

Fear not, for I have redeemed you [ransomed you by paying a price instead of leaving you captives]; I have called you by your name; you are Mine. When you pass through the waters, I will be with you, and through the rivers, they will not overwhelm you. When you walk through the fire, you will not be burned or scorched, nor will the flame kindle upon you. For I am the Lord your God, the Holy One of Israel, your Savior.

Psalm 34:18, NKJV

The LORD is near to those who have a broken heart, and saves such as have a contrite spirit.

Psalm 147:3, AMP

He heals the brokenhearted and binds up their wounds [curing their pains and their sorrows].

Psalm 3:3, AMP

But You, O Lord, are a shield for me, my glory, and the lifter of my head.

Deuteronomy 33:27, NKJV

"The eternal God is your refuge, and underneath are the everlasting arms."

30. Completely Filled in Christ

In Christ, I am complete—I have received of His fullness. I am ever being filled with the Spirit. I am filled with His love. I am filled with the knowledge of His will. I am filled with the humility of Jesus. I am filled with fruits of righteousness. I am filled with joy, peace, and hope.

Colossians 2:9, 10, NIV

In Christ all the fullness of the Deity lives in bodily form, and you have been given fullness in Christ, who is the head over every power and authority.

John 1:16, AMP

Out of His fullness (abundance) we have all received [all had a share and we were all supplied with] one grace after another and spiritual blessing upon spiritual blessing and even favor upon favor and gift [heaped] upon gift.

Ephesians 5:18, AMP

Ever be filled and stimulated with the [Holy] Spirit.

Romans 5:5, AMP

God's love has been poured out in our hearts through the Holy Spirit Who has been given to us.

Colossians 1:9, 10, NASB

Ask that you may be filled with the knowledge of His will in all spiritual wisdom and understanding, so that you will walk in a manner worthy of the Lord.

Philippians 2:5–8, NKJV

Let this mind be in you which was also in Christ Jesus. . . . He humbled Himself and became obedient to the point of death, even the death of the cross.

Philippians 1:9–11, NKJV

This I pray, that your love may abound still more and more in knowledge and all discernment, that you may approve the things that are excellent . . . being filled with the fruits of righteousness which are by Jesus Christ, to the glory and praise of God.

Romans 15:13, NIV

May the God of hope fill you with all joy and peace as you trust in him, so that you may overflow with hope by the power of the Holy Spirit.

31. Confusion to Peace

When the enemy tries to cloud my mind with confusion, I pull out my sword and say—It is written! God is not the author of confusion and disorder, but of peace and order. I have not been given a spirit of fear. God has given me a spirit of power and of love and of sound mind. God is righteous—He has cut me free from the cords of the wicked.

By His Word and His Spirit, I am filled with the wisdom that is from above. I put my life in order by what He has taught me. I avoid envy and self-seeking, which are rooted in confusion and evil. God gives me purity in thought, peaceable actions, and a gentle spirit that is willing to yield, full of mercy and good fruits. I sow His seeds of righteousness in peace, by making peace with those around me.

1 Corinthians 14:33, NKJV

God is not the author of confusion but of peace.

2 Timothy 1:7, NKJV

God has not given us a spirit of fear, but of power and of love and of a sound mind.

Psalm 129:4, NIV

The LORD is righteous; he has cut me free from the cords of the wicked.

Philippians 3:16, AMP

Only let us hold true to what we have already attained and walk and order our lives by that.

James 3:16–18, NKJV

For where envy and self-seeking exist, confusion and every evil thing are there. But the wisdom that is from above is first pure, then peaceable, gentle, willing to yield, full of mercy and good fruits, without partiality and without hypocrisy. Now the fruit of righteousness is sown in peace by those who make peace.

2 Corinthians 13:11, AMP

Be strengthened (perfected, completed, made what you ought to be); be encouraged and consoled and comforted; be of the same [agreeable] mind one with another; live in peace, and [then] the God of love [Who is the Source of affection, goodwill, love, and benevolence toward men] and the Author and Promoter of peace will be with you.

Romans 12:18, AMP

If possible, as far as it depends on you, live at peace with everyone.

32. Consequences of My Sin

Holy and righteous Father, I know You do not willingly grieve me—but You allow me to suffer the consequences of my sin to teach me lessons that result in my eternal benefit. You are aware of the path of sin. If, when I am tempted, I allow unrighteous desire to be conceived in me, it gives birth to sin—and if I allow sin to become full-grown, it brings forth death. My rebellion against Your Word leaves me empty, wounded, and bound.

Yet, You are moved by compassion according to Your tender mercy, which endures forever. I cry out to You in my trouble, and You deliver me from my distress. You satisfy my longing soul. You fill my hungry soul with goodness. You break the chains of sin that bind me and send Your Word to heal me.

Thank You, Lord, for delivering me from my destruction. I will always remember Your goodness and give thanks for Your wonderful works toward me.

Lamentations 3:32, 33, AMP

Though He causes grief, yet will He be moved to compassion according to the multitude of His loving-kindness and tender mercy. For He does not willingly and from His heart afflict or grieve the children of men.

James 1:13–15, NKJV

Let no one say when he is tempted, "I am tempted by God"; for God cannot be tempted by evil, nor does He Himself tempt anyone. But each one is tempted when he is drawn away by his own desires and enticed. Then, when desire has conceived, it gives birth to sin; and sin, when it is full-grown, brings forth death.

Psalm 107:1, 6, 9–14, 20, 21, NKJV

Oh, give thanks to the LORD, for He is good! For His mercy endures forever.
They cried out to the LORD in their trouble, and He delivered them out of their distresses.
. . . He satisfies the longing soul, and fills the hungry soul with goodness. Those who sat in darkness and in the shadow of death, bound in affliction and irons—because they rebelled against the words of God, and despised the counsel of the Most High, therefore He brought down their heart with labor; they fell down, and there was none to help. Then they cried out to the LORD in their trouble, and He saved them out of their distresses. He brought them out of darkness and the shadow of death, and broke their chains in pieces.
. . . He sent His word and healed them, and delivered them from their destructions. Oh, that men would give thanks to the LORD for His goodness, and for His wonderful works to the children of men!

33. Contentment in Christ

In Christ, I am content—no matter what my circumstances. I can face any problem with a cheerful attitude, because Christ walks with me through every situation and gives me strength to handle it.

Godliness accompanied with contentment is my means of achieving victory. I will not fall into the devil's snare of coveting riches and always wanting more. I'd rather have Jesus than anything this world has to offer. He is my helper, so why should I fear or be dissatisfied?

Thank You, Lord, for the gift of contentment! What peace it brings! I am thankful, Lord, for the good inheritance I have in You!

Philippians 4:11–13, NASB

I have learned to be content in whatever circumstances I am. I know how to get along with humble means, and I also know how to live in prosperity; in any and every circumstance I have learned the secret of being filled and going hungry, both of having abundance and suffering need. I can do all things through Him who strengthens me.

1 Timothy 6:6–10, NKJV

Godliness with contentment is great gain. For we brought nothing into this world, and it is certain we can carry nothing out. And having food and clothing, with these we shall be content. But those who desire to be rich fall into temptation and a snare, and into many foolish and harmful lusts which drown men in destruction and perdition. For the love of money is a root of all kinds of evil, for which some have strayed from the faith in their greediness, and pierced themselves through with many sorrows.

Proverbs 16:8, AMP

Better is a little with righteousness (uprightness in every area and relation and right standing with God) than great revenues with injustice.

Ecclesiastes 4:6, AMP

Better is a handful with quietness than both hands full with painful effort, a vain striving after the wind and a feeding on it.

Hebrews 13:5, 6, NASB

Make sure that your character is free from the love of money, being content with what you have; for He Himself has said, "I will never desert you, nor will I ever forsake you," so that we confidently say, "The Lord is my helper, I will not be afraid. What will man do to me?"

34. Crucified With Christ

I am crucified with Christ! I live my life by faith in Jesus, Who loved me and gave Himself up for me. Daily I die to self. Day by day, I choose to pick up my cross. By the power of the Holy Spirit, I put to death the deeds of my sinful nature. My flesh is crucified; I live by the Spirit.

God forbid that I should boast except in what Jesus has done to save me. It is by Him that the world is crucified to me, and I to the world. I have died to the ways of this world system. My real life is hidden with Christ in God!

Galatians 2:20, NASB

"I have been crucified with Christ; and it is no longer I who live, but Christ lives in me; and the life which I now live in the flesh I live by faith in the Son of God, who loved me and gave Himself up for me."

1 Corinthians 15:31, AMP

I die daily [I face death every day and die to self].

Luke 9:23, NKJV

"If anyone desires to come after Me, let him deny himself, and take up his cross daily, and follow Me."

Romans 8:13, NKJV

If you live according to the flesh you will die; but if by the Spirit you put to death the deeds of the body, you will live.

Galatians 5:24, 25, AMP

And those who belong to Christ Jesus (the Messiah) have crucified the flesh (the godless human nature) with its passions and appetites and desires. If we live by the [Holy] Spirit, let us also walk by the Spirit.

Galatians 6:14, NKJV

God forbid that I should boast except in the cross of our Lord Jesus Christ, by whom the world has been crucified to me, and I to the world.

Colossians 3:3, NIV

For you died, and your life is now hidden with Christ in God.

35. Curses Turned to Blessings

I am walking in God's purpose for my life. Because He loves me, He turns my curses into blessings. I am blessed in my going out (my beginning) and my coming in (my finishing).

Thank You, Lord, for turning my weeping into dancing. Thank You for comforting me—for giving me beauty and the oil of joy. You have taken away my spirit of heaviness and replaced it with the garment of praise. I am rooted in Your righteousness, and You have made me glad.

Deuteronomy 23:5, NASB

"The LORD your God turned the curse into a blessing for you because the LORD your God loves you."

Proverbs 26:2, NIV

Like a fluttering sparrow or a darting swallow, an undeserved curse does not come to rest.

Psalm 121:8, NKJV

The LORD shall preserve your going out and your coming in from this time forth, and even forevermore.

Deuteronomy 28:6, 7, AMP

Blessed shall you be when you come in and blessed shall you be when you go out. The Lord shall cause your enemies who rise up against you to be defeated before your face; they shall come out against you one way and flee before you seven ways.

Psalm 30:5, 11, AMP

His anger is but for a moment, but His favor is for a lifetime or in His favor is life. Weeping may endure for a night, but joy comes in the morning. . . . You have turned my mourning into dancing for me; You have put off my sackcloth and girded me with gladness.

Isaiah 61:2, 3, NKJV

"To proclaim the acceptable year of the LORD, and the day of vengeance of our God; to comfort all who mourn, to console those who mourn in Zion, to give them beauty for ashes, the oil of joy for mourning, the garment of praise for the spirit of heaviness; that they may be called trees of righteousness, the planting of the LORD, that He may be glorified."

36. Cut Free From the Cords of the Wicked

I am the redeemed of the Lord. He has cut me free from the cord of the wicked that once bound me. He has opened my eyes and turned me from darkness to light—releasing me from Satan's power and causing me to draw on God's power.

I belong to God. He calls me by my name. No matter what the enemy throws at me, I know that I will come through victorious on the other side. When I fall, I will arise. When darkness surrounds me, the Lord will be a light to me.

God goes with me. I am confident He will never fail me nor forsake me.

Psalm 107:2, NKJV

Let the redeemed of the LORD say so, whom He has redeemed from the hand of the enemy.

Psalm 129:4, NIV

The LORD is righteous; he has cut me free from the cords of the wicked.

Acts 26:18, NKJV

"To open their eyes and turn them from darkness to light, and from the power of Satan to God, that they may receive forgiveness of sins and an inheritance among those who are sanctified by faith in Me."

Isaiah 43:1–3, NKJV

"Fear not, for I have redeemed you; I have called you by your name; you are Mine. When you pass through the waters, I will be with you; and through the rivers, they shall not overflow you. When you walk through the fire, you shall not be burned, nor shall the flame scorch you. For I am the LORD your God, the Holy One of Israel, your Savior."

Micah 7:8, NKJV

Do not rejoice over me, my enemy; when I fall, I will arise; when I sit in darkness, the LORD will be a light to me.

Deuteronomy 31:6, NASB

"Be strong and courageous, do not be afraid or tremble at them, for the LORD your God is the one who goes with you. He will not fail you or forsake you."

37. Dead to Sin—Alive to God

When the tempter tries to trip me and entangle my feet in his snare, I pull out my sword and say—**It is written!** I am dead to sin, but alive to God. I am under the power of His grace, and sin shall not be my master.

I have put on Christ, and I will make no provision for my flesh. God has given me the victory through my Lord Jesus Christ. Hallelujah!

I have received an abundance of grace and the gift of righteousness, and—through Christ—I will reign in life.

Romans 6:11, NASB

Consider yourselves to be dead to sin, but alive to God in Christ Jesus.

Romans 6:14, NIV

Sin shall not be your master, because you are not under law, but under grace.

Romans 13:14, NKJV

Put on the Lord Jesus Christ, and make no provision for the flesh, to fulfill its lusts.

1 Corinthians 15:57, NIV

Thanks be to God! He gives us the victory through our Lord Jesus Christ.

Romans 5:17, NKJV

For if by the one man's offense death reigned through the one, much more those who receive abundance of grace and of the gift of righteousness will reign in life through the One, Jesus Christ.

38. The Desires of Your Heart

My desire is to reveal His love and power, to exalt His Word and His Name, and to bring glory to Jesus Christ—the risen and exalted One. To protect His righteous reputation and make known His lavish love, I walk in the way of His laws as I wait for Him.

I delight myself in the Lord! The more time I spend in His Word, the more His thoughts become my thoughts. He gives me the desires of my heart, because His desires have become my desires. I submit and commit my way to my perfect Father—trusting in Him. Because they line up with His perfect will, He fulfills my desires.

Psalm 138:1, 2, AMP

I will confess and praise You [O God] with my whole heart. . . . I will worship toward Your holy temple and praise Your name for Your loving-kindness and Your truth and faithfulness; for You have exalted above all else Your name and Your word and You have magnified Your word above all Your name!

Isaiah 26:8, NIV

Yes, Lord, walking in the way of your laws, we wait for you; your name and renown are the desire of our hearts.

Psalm 37:4, 5, NASB

Delight yourself in the Lord; and He will give you the desires of your heart. Commit your way to the Lord, trust also in Him, and He will do it.

39. Destroying Double-Minded Doubt

I am not double minded. I do not anger God by speaking in doubt against Him and His ability to perform His Word. Without faith it is impossible to please God, and no wonder—to doubt God's Word is the same as accusing Him of being a liar!

I have no doubt regarding His promises. He strengthens my faith. I am fully persuaded that He has the awesome power to do everything He has promised and more. I know my God, in whom I trust, is able to protect and perform the work He has commissioned me to do. I am persuaded He is able to keep my salvation and eternal future until His second coming. To God be the glory!

James 1:6–8, NKJV

Let him ask in faith, with no doubting, for he who doubts is like a wave of the sea driven and tossed by the wind. For let not that man suppose that he will receive anything from the Lord; he is a double-minded man, unstable in all his ways.

Psalm 78:19–22, AMP

Yes, they spoke against God; They said, **Can God** furnish [the food for] a table in the wilderness? Behold, He did smite the rock so that waters gushed out and the streams overflowed; **but can He** give bread also? **Can He** provide flesh for His people? Therefore when the LORD heard, He was [full of] wrath . . . because in God they believed not [they relied not on Him, they adhered not to Him], and they trusted not in His salvation (His power to save).

Hebrews 11:6, AMP

Without faith it is impossible to please and be satisfactory to Him. For whoever would come near to God must [necessarily] believe that God exists and that He is the rewarder of those who earnestly and diligently seek Him [out].

1 John 5:10, NIV

Anyone who does not believe God has made him out to be a liar, because he has not believed the testimony God has given.

Romans 4:20, 21, NIV

He did not waver through unbelief regarding the promise of God, but was strengthened in his faith and gave glory to God, being fully persuaded that God had power to do what he had promised.

40. Draw Near to God

Through His Spirit and His Word, and with a heart filled with passion, God has wooed me by His infinite love. I draw near to Him and—as He promised—He draws near to me. As I submit my life to God, He gives me the power to resist evil, and the devil must flee from me. I am assured that God will never leave me nor forsake me. With extreme confidence, I declare that the Lord is my helper. I will not fear. I rest in His everlasting arms, and He thrusts out the enemy before me.

Jeremiah 31:3, NKJV

The LORD has appeared of old to me, saying, "Yes, I have loved you with an everlasting love; therefore with lovingkindness I have drawn you."

James 4:7, 8, NKJV

Therefore submit to God. Resist the devil and he will flee from you. Draw near to God and He will draw near to you.

Hebrews 13:5, 6, NKJV

For He Himself has said, "I will never leave you nor forsake you." So we may boldly say: "The Lord is my helper; I will not fear. What can man do to me?"

Deuteronomy 33:27, NIV

"The eternal God is your refuge, and underneath are the everlasting arms. He will drive out your enemy before you, saying, 'Destroy him!' "

41. Earnestly Seek God

I am an earnest seeker of God. I am passionate over the One who is passionate over me. I study His Word, meditating on His message of love. Knowing my identity "in Christ" and knowing my heavenly Father by experience are my top priority.

With all of my heart, I seek His face and an increased intimacy in our relationship. His love is better than life, and my desire is to understand His magnificent love. I practice His presence in earnest awareness that He is always with me. I spend intense times pouring out my heart in prayer. I concentrate on pleasing Him by earnestly obeying His commandments. He gives His Spirit to those who obey Him, and I want more of His Spirit.

I am receiving a reward for my passionate and earnest efforts.

Psalm 63:1–4, NIV

O God, you are my God, **earnestly I seek you;** my soul thirsts for you, my body longs for you, in a dry and weary land where there is no water. I have seen you in the sanctuary and beheld your power and your glory. Because your love is better than life, my lips will glorify you. I will praise you as long as I live, and in your name I will lift up my hands.

Jeremiah 29:12–14, NKJV

You will call upon Me and go and pray to Me, and I will listen to you. And you will seek Me and find Me, when you **search for Me with all your heart.** I will be found by you, says the LORD, and I will bring you back from your captivity.

Hebrews 13:5, NIV

God has said, "Never will I leave you; never will I forsake you."

Deuteronomy 11:13, 14, NKJV

"It shall be that if you diligently **obey My commandments** which I command you today, to love the LORD your God and serve Him with all your heart and with all your soul, then I will give you the rain for your land in its season, the early rain and the latter rain."

Acts 5:32, NKJV

"We are His witnesses to these things, and so also is the Holy Spirit whom God has given to those who obey Him."

Hebrews 11:6, NIV

Without faith it is impossible to please God, because anyone who comes to him must believe that he exists and that he rewards those who earnestly seek him.

42. Equipped to Do His Will

In Christ Jesus, I have already been blessed with every spiritual blessing and equipped with everything good for doing God's will and pleasing Him in every way. God is working to teach me His will and cause me to desire that His will be done.

I must turn my willingness into resolve. The Lord does not force me to act.

I must take that first "step of faith" and then the power of God shows up to cause me to act according to His good purposes.

My life is dedicated to the Lord. Still, I fully recognize that I might fail to dedicate each day to Him. Day by day, I must make a conscious choice to walk with Him.

Ephesians 1:3, NIV

Praise be to the God and Father of our Lord Jesus Christ, who has blessed us in the heavenly realms with every spiritual blessing in Christ.

2 Peter 1:3, 4, NIV

His divine power has given us everything we need for life and godliness through our knowledge of him who called us by his own glory and goodness. Through these he has given us his very great and precious promises, so that through them you may participate in the divine nature and escape the corruption in the world caused by evil desires.

Hebrews 13:20, 21, NKJV

Now may the God of peace who brought up our Lord Jesus from the dead, that great Shepherd of the sheep, through the blood of the everlasting covenant, make you complete in every good work to do His will, working in you what is well pleasing in His sight, through Jesus Christ, to whom be glory forever and ever. Amen.

1 Thessalonians 5:23, 24, NKJV

Now may the God of peace Himself sanctify you completely; and may your whole spirit, soul, and body be preserved blameless at the coming of our Lord Jesus Christ. He who calls you is faithful, who also will do it.

Philippians 2:13, NKJV

It is God who works in you both to will and to do for His good pleasure.

Joshua 24:15, NKJV

"Choose for yourselves this day whom you will serve."

43. Faith—the Essential Factor

Loving Father, I know to doubt Your promises is to regard You as a liar. Without faith, I cannot be pleasing to You. Oh, Lord, I know You exist and You reward those who earnestly seek You.

Faith without works is dead. Disobedience (unbelief) is a sin that keeps me from entering Your promises. Your message is of no value to me unless I combine the message with actions of faith. I know this, Lord.

Oh, Father, I believe—help my unbelief! Increase my faith. Make it as a mustard seed that starts small, but has the potential to accomplish great works.

1 John 5:10, NASB

The one who does not believe God has made Him a liar, because he has not believed in the testimony that God has given.

Hebrews 11:6, NIV

Without faith it is impossible to please God, because anyone who comes to him must believe that he exists and that he rewards those who earnestly seek him.

James 2:19, 20, NKJV

You believe that there is one God. You do well. Even the demons believe—and tremble! But do you want to know, O foolish man, that faith without works is dead?

Hebrews 3:17–19, NKJV

Now with whom was He angry forty years? Was it not with those who sinned, whose corpses fell in the wilderness? And to whom did He swear that they would not enter His rest, but to those who did not obey? So we see that they could not enter in because of unbelief.

Hebrews 4:2, AMP

Indeed we have had the glad tidings [Gospel of God] proclaimed to us just as truly as they [the Israelites of old did when the good news of deliverance from bondage came to them]; **but the message they heard did not benefit them, because it was not mixed with faith** . . . by those who heard it.

Mark 9:23, 24, NKJV

"If you can believe, all things are possible to him who believes." Immediately the father of the child cried out . . . , "Lord, I believe; help my unbelief!"

44. Faith Honors God—God Honors Faith

My faith brings glory to God. I am blessed because I believe what God has promised, He will also accomplish. God is the object of my faith! His faithfulness to His Word is the firm foundation of my faith.

My faith honors God—God honors my faith! Because I believe, I will see the glory of God revealed. Great is His faithfulness!

Romans 4:20–22, NKJV

He did not waver at the promise of God through unbelief, but was strengthened in faith, giving glory to God, and being fully convinced that what He had promised He was also able to perform. And therefore "it was accounted to him for righteousness."

Luke 1:45, NIV

"Blessed is she who has believed that what the Lord has said to her will be accomplished!"

Psalm 89:33, 34, NKJV

"My lovingkindness I will not utterly take from him, nor allow My faithfulness to fail. My covenant I will not break, nor alter the word that has gone out of My lips."

Matthew 9:28–30, NASB

When He entered the house, the blind men came up to Him, and Jesus said to them, "Do you believe that I am able to do this?" They said to Him, "Yes, Lord." Then He touched their eyes, saying, "It shall be done to you according to your faith." And their eyes were opened.

Matthew 8:10–13, NASB

"Truly I say to you, I have not found such great faith with anyone in Israel". . . . And Jesus said to the centurion, "Go; it shall be done for you as you have believed." And the servant was healed that very moment.

Matthew 15:28, NKJV

Then Jesus answered and said to her, "O woman, great is your faith! Let it be to you as you desire." And her daughter was healed from that very hour.

John 11:40, NKJV

Jesus said to her, "Did I not say to you that if you would believe you would see the glory of God?"

45. Fear Not—God Quiets My Fears

I do not fear, for He is with me. I am not discouraged, for He is my God. He strengthens me, helps me, and upholds me in His everlasting arms. He calls me by my name—I am His, and He is mine! The Lord is my strength and my shield. He protects me, and He is mighty to save.

Holy and righteous Lord, thank You for quieting my fears with Your love. When I sought You, You answered and delivered me from all my fears.

Isaiah 41:10, NKJV

" 'Fear not, for I am with you; be not dismayed, for I am your God. I will strengthen you, Yes, I will help you, I will uphold you with My righteous right hand.' "

Deuteronomy 33:27, NIV

"The eternal God is your refuge, and underneath are the everlasting arms. He will drive out your enemy before you, saying, 'Destroy him!' "

Isaiah 43:1–3, NKJV

"Fear not, for I have redeemed you; I have called you by your name; You are Mine. When you pass through the waters, I will be with you; and through the rivers, they shall not overflow you. When you walk through the fire, you shall not be burned, nor shall the flame scorch you. For I am the LORD your God, the Holy One of Israel, your Savior."

Psalm 28:7, NKJV

The LORD is my strength and my shield; my heart trusted in Him, and I am helped; therefore my heart greatly rejoices, and with my song I will praise Him.

Zephaniah 3:16, 17, NKJV

"Do not fear, . . . let not your hands be weak. The LORD your God in your midst, the Mighty One, will save; He will rejoice over you with gladness; He will quiet you in His love; He will rejoice over you with singing."

Psalm 57:1, AMP

BE MERCIFUL and gracious to me, O God, be merciful and gracious to me, for my soul takes refuge and finds shelter and confidence in You; yes, in the shadow of Your wings will I take refuge and be confident until calamities and destructive storms are passed.

Psalm 34:4, NASB

I sought the LORD, and He answered me, and delivered me from all my fears.

46. Finishing by God's Grace

By God's grace, I am a good finisher and not just good at beginning things. I consider the cost before I commit to do something. I do not despise the day of small beginnings. Whatever I find to do, I do it with all my heart. I finish what I have committed to do, according to my ability and means.

I have put my hand to the plow, and I will not look back. God has cupped His hand over mine. By His grace, I will finish the race of faith with joy. I strip off every unnecessary weight and lay aside the sin that so easily entangles me—and, keeping my eyes fixed on Jesus—I run with endurance.

Forgetting what is in the past, I press forward toward the heavenly prize. The Lord will perfect His work in me; I lack no spiritual gift. He will keep me strong to the end, so that I will be blameless on the day of my Lord Jesus Christ. I will keep the faith and finish the race—by His grace.

Luke 14:28–30, NKJV

"For which of you, intending to build a tower, does not sit down first and count the cost, whether he has enough to finish it—lest, after he has laid the foundation, and is not able to finish it, all who see it begin to mock him, saying, 'This man began to build and was not able to finish.' "

Zechariah 4:10, NASB

"Who has despised the day of small things?"

Ecclesiastes 9:10, AMP

Whatever your hand finds to do, do it with all your might, for there is no work or device or knowledge or wisdom in Sheol (the place of the dead), where you are going.

2 Corinthians 8:11, 12, AMP

So now finish doing it, that your [enthusiastic] readiness in desiring it may be equaled by your completion of it according to your ability and means. For if the [eager] readiness to give is there, then it is acceptable and welcomed in proportion to what a person has, not according to what he does not have.

Luke 9:62, AMP

Jesus said to him, No one who puts his hand to the plow and looks back [to the things behind] is fit for the kingdom of God.

Acts 20:24, NKJV

"Nor do I count my life dear to myself, so that I may finish my race with joy, and the ministry which I received from the Lord Jesus, to testify to the gospel of the grace of God."

Hebrews 12:1, 2, NKJV

Let us lay aside every weight, and the sin which so easily ensnares us, and let us run with endurance the race that is set before us, looking unto Jesus, the author and finisher of our faith.

Philippians 3:12–14, NASB

Not that I have already obtained it or have already become perfect, but I press on so that I may lay hold of that for which also I was laid hold of by Christ Jesus. Brethren, I do not regard myself as having laid hold of it yet; but one thing I do: forgetting what lies behind and reaching forward to what lies ahead, I press on toward the goal for the prize of the upward call of God in Christ Jesus.

Psalm 138:8, NKJV

The LORD will perfect that which concerns me; Your mercy, O LORD, endures forever; do not forsake the works of Your hands.

1 Corinthians 1:7, 8, NIV

You do not lack any spiritual gift as you eagerly wait for our Lord Jesus Christ to be revealed. He will keep you strong to the end, so that you will be blameless on the day of our Lord Jesus Christ.

2 Timothy 4:7, NIV

I have fought the good fight, I have finished the race, I have kept the faith.

47. Focus on the Eternal

I focus my mind on eternal, spiritual matters—not on the temporary, physical things of this world. My sin nature has been put to death, and I find my real life hidden with Christ in God.

Fixing my eyes on Jesus—the author and finisher of my faith—I deny ungodliness and worldly lusts. I look for the blessed hope and glorious second coming of my Lord! I sow to the Spirit to reap everlasting life, remaining in Christ and in the Father. His promise to me is eternal life.

2 Corinthians 4:17, 18, NIV

Our light and momentary troubles are achieving for us an eternal glory that far outweighs them all. So we fix our eyes not on what is seen, but on what is unseen. For what is seen is temporary, but what is unseen is eternal.

Colossians 3:2, 3, AMP

Set your minds and keep them set on what is above (the higher things), not on the things that are on the earth. For [as far as this world is concerned] you have died, and your [new, real] life is hidden with Christ in God.

Hebrews 12:2, NASB

Fixing our eyes on Jesus, the author and perfecter of faith, who for the joy set before Him endured the cross, despising the shame, and has sat down at the right hand of the throne of God.

Titus 2:11–14, NKJV

For the grace of God that brings salvation has appeared to all men, teaching us that, denying ungodliness and worldly lusts, we should live soberly, righteously, and godly in the present age, looking for the blessed hope and glorious appearing of our great God and Savior Jesus Christ, who gave Himself for us, that He might redeem us from every lawless deed and purify for Himself His own special people, zealous for good works.

Galatians 6:7, 8, NKJV

Do not be deceived, God is not mocked; for whatever a man sows, that he will also reap. For he who sows to his flesh will of the flesh reap corruption, but he who sows to the Spirit will of the Spirit reap everlasting life.

48. Forgiven and Cleansed of All Unrighteousness

With a humble heart, I daily confess my sins. In sincere repentance and turning away from sin, I am forgiven. The blood of Christ cleanses me of all unrighteousness—God washes me thoroughly and repeatedly from the stain of my guilt and makes me white as snow.

He cancels and blots out my transgressions for His own sake. As far as the east is from the west, so far has He removed my transgressions from me.

His grace is sufficient to cover all my sins and He remembers them no more.

Ezekiel 18:21, 22, NKJV

"If a wicked man turns from all his sins . . . keeps all My statutes, and does what is lawful and right, he shall surely live; he shall not die. **None** of the transgressions which he has committed shall be remembered against him."

1 John 1:7–9, NKJV

If we walk in the light as He is in the light, . . . the blood of Jesus Christ His Son cleanses us from all sin. If we say that we have no sin, we deceive ourselves, and the truth is not in us. **If we confess our sins, He is faithful and just to forgive us our sins and to cleanse us from all unrighteousness.**

Revelation 1:5, NKJV

Jesus Christ, the faithful witness, the firstborn from the dead, and the ruler over the kings of the earth. To Him who loved us and washed us from our sins in His own blood.

Ephesians 1:7, NKJV

In Him we have redemption through His blood, the forgiveness of sins, according to the riches of His grace.

Revelation 7:14, NASB

"These are the ones who come out of the great tribulation, and they have washed their robes and made them white in the blood of the Lamb."

Psalm 51:2–7, AMP

Wash me thoroughly [and repeatedly] from my iniquity and guilt and cleanse me and make me wholly pure from my sin! For I am conscious of my transgressions and I acknowledge them; my sin is ever before me. . . . Wash me, and I shall [in reality] be whiter than snow.

Isaiah 1:18, NASB

"Come now, and let us reason together," Says the LORD, "Though your sins are as scarlet, they will be as white as snow."

Hebrews 8:10–12, NIV

"This is the covenant. . . . I will put my laws in their minds and write them on their hearts. I will be their God, and they will be my people. . . . They will all know me. . . . **I will forgive their wickedness and will remember their sins no more.**"

Isaiah 43:25, AMP

I, even I, am He Who blots out and cancels your transgressions, for My own sake, and **I will not remember** your sins.

Isaiah 44:22, NKJV

"I have blotted out, like a thick cloud, your transgressions, and like a cloud, your sins. Return to Me, for I have redeemed you."

Psalm 103:12, NKJV

As far as the east is from the west, so far has He removed our transgressions from us.

2 Corinthians 12:9, NIV

"My grace is sufficient for you."

1 Kings 14:8, NKJV

"You have not been as My servant David, who kept My commandments and who followed Me with all his heart, to do only what was right in My eyes." *(Author's note: God spoke this after David's death, demonstrating that the Lord forgot the sins David asked Him to forgive).*

49. Freely Forgive Others—Pray for Your Enemies

I freely forgive others and I pray for my enemies. I do not return evil for evil or insult for insult. I no longer regard anyone from an earthly point of view. I strive to see everyone from God's perspective. Remembering how much He has forgiven me helps me to forgive others from my heart. I am commanded to live in love, because **"God is Love."** Lord, pour Your love for others into my heart.

Colossians 3:13, AMP

Even as the Lord has [freely] forgiven you, so must you also [forgive].

Matthew 5:44–48; 6:14, NIV

"Love your enemies and pray for those who persecute you, that you may be sons of your Father in heaven. . . . If you love those who love you, what reward will you get? Are not even the tax collectors doing that? . . . Be perfect, therefore, as your heavenly Father is perfect." . . . "If you forgive men when they sin against you, your heavenly Father will also forgive you."

1 Peter 3:9, NIV

Do not repay evil with evil or insult with insult, but with blessing, because to this you were called so that you may inherit a blessing.

Colossians 3:12, 13, NIV

Clothe yourselves with compassion, kindness, humility, gentleness and patience. **Bear with each other and forgive** whatever grievances you may have against one another. **Forgive as the Lord forgave you.**

Mark 11:25, 26, AMP

Whenever you stand praying, if you have anything against anyone, forgive him and let it drop (leave it, let it go), in order that your Father Who is in heaven may also forgive you your [own] failings and shortcomings and let them drop. But if you do not forgive, neither will your Father in heaven forgive your failings and shortcomings.

1 John 4:7–12, NKJV

Beloved, let us love one another, for love is of God; and everyone who loves is born of God and knows God. He who does not love does not know God, for God is love. In this the love of God was manifested toward us, that God has sent His only begotten Son into the world, that we might live through Him. In this is love, not that we loved God, but that

He loved us and sent His Son to be the propitiation for our sins. Beloved, if God so loved us, we also ought to love one another. No one has seen God at any time. If we love one another, God abides in us, and His love has been perfected in us.

2 Corinthians 5:16, NIV
From now on we regard no one from a worldly point of view.

Matthew 18:22–35, NIV
Jesus answered, . . . "Therefore, the kingdom of heaven is like a king who wanted to settle accounts with his servants. As he began the settlement, a man who owed him ten thousand talents was brought to him. Since he was not able to pay, the master ordered . . . all that he had be sold to repay the debt. The servant fell on his knees. . . . 'Be patient with me,' he begged, 'and I will pay back everything.' The servant's master took pity on him, canceled the debt and let him go. But when that servant went out, he found one of his fellow servants who owed him a hundred denarii. He grabbed him and began to choke him. 'Pay back what you owe me!' he demanded. His fellow servant fell to his knees and begged him, 'Be patient with me, and I will pay you back.' But he refused. Instead, he went off and had the man thrown into prison until he could pay the debt. When the other servants saw what had happened, they . . . went and told their master everything. . . . Then the master called the servant in. 'You wicked servant,' he said, 'I canceled all that debt of yours because you begged me to. Shouldn't you have had mercy on your fellow servant just as I had on you?' In anger his master turned him over to the jailers to be tortured, until he should pay back all he owed. **This is how my heavenly Father will treat each of you unless you forgive your brother from your heart.**"

1 John 4:16–21, NASB
We have come to know and have believed the love which God has for us. God is love, and the one who abides in love abides in God, and God abides in him. By this, love is perfected with us, so that we may have confidence in the day of judgment; because as He is, so also are we in this world. There is no fear in love; but perfect love casts out fear, because fear involves punishment, and the one who fears is not perfected in love. We love, because He first loved us. If someone says, "I love God," and hates his brother, he is a liar; for the one who does not love his brother whom he has seen, cannot love God whom he has not seen. And this commandment we have from Him, that the one who loves God should love his brother also.

Romans 5:5, NKJV
Hope does not disappoint, because the love of God has been poured out in our hearts by the Holy Spirit who was given to us.

50. The Furnace of Affliction

As I am tested in the furnace of affliction, I praise God for the refining work He is accomplishing in my life. I can count on this—the fiery trials through which God permits me to pass result in my eternal benefit (or else He would not allow them).

I have a living hope in the inheritance God has reserved for me in heaven. I know I am kept by His power through faith for eternal life with Him. The Lord tests my heart through the crucible of adversity, but He preserves my life and keeps my feet from slipping. By His grace, this testing will cause me to come forth as pure gold.

Isaiah 48:10, NASB

"Behold, I have refined you, but not as silver; I have tested you in the furnace of affliction."

1 Peter 4:12, 13, NKJV

Beloved, do not think it strange concerning the fiery trial which is to try you, as though some strange thing happened to you; but rejoice to the extent that you partake of Christ's sufferings, that when His glory is revealed, you may also be glad with exceeding joy.

1 Peter 1:3–9, NKJV

Blessed be the God and Father of our Lord Jesus Christ, who according to His abundant mercy has begotten us again to a living hope through the resurrection of Jesus Christ from the dead, to an inheritance incorruptible and undefiled and that does not fade away, reserved in heaven for you, who are kept by the power of God through faith for salvation ready to be revealed in the last time. In this you greatly rejoice, though now for a little while, if need be, you have been grieved by various trials, that the genuineness of your faith, being much more precious than gold that perishes, though it is tested by fire, may be found to praise, honor, and glory at the revelation of Jesus Christ, whom having not seen you love. Though now you do not see Him, yet believing, you rejoice with joy inexpressible and full of glory, receiving the end of your faith—the salvation of your souls.

Malachi 3:3, NKJV

"He will sit as a refiner and a purifier of silver; He will purify the sons of Levi, and purge them as gold and silver, that they may offer to the LORD an offering in righteousness."

Psalm 66:9, 10, NIV

He has preserved our lives and kept our feet from slipping. For you, O God, tested us; you refined us like silver.

51. God Defends My Cause

God vigorously defends my cause. I am still before Him, and He makes the justice of my cause shine like the noonday sun.

He contends with those who contend with me. No weapon formed against me will prosper or prevail. He opens doors no one can shut—He closes doors that no one can open.

My Lord performs on my behalf. If God is for me, who can be against me?

Jeremiah 50:34, AMP

Their Redeemer is strong; the Lord of hosts is His name. He will surely **and thoroughly plead their case and defend their cause.**

Psalm 37:6, 7, NIV

He will make your righteousness shine like the dawn, the justice of your cause like the noonday sun. Be still before the LORD and wait patiently for him.

Isaiah 49:25, NKJV

Thus says the LORD: . . . "I will contend with him who contends with you."

Isaiah 54:17, AMP

No weapon that is formed against you shall prosper, and every tongue that shall rise against you in judgment you shall show to be in the wrong. This [peace, righteousness, security, triumph over opposition] is the heritage of the servants of the LORD [those in whom the ideal Servant of the Lord is reproduced].

Revelation 3:7, 8, NKJV

"These things says He who is holy, He who is true, 'He who has the key of David, He who opens and no one shuts, and shuts and no one opens': I know your works. See, I have set before you an open door, and no one can shut it; for you have a little strength, have kept My word, and have not denied My name."

Psalm 57:2, AMP

I will cry to God Most High, **Who performs on my behalf** and rewards me [Who brings to pass His purposes for me and surely completes them]!

Romans 8:31, NIV

What, then, shall we say in response to this? If God is for us, who can be against us?

52. God Has a Plan for Your Life—Seek Him Earnestly

Heavenly Father, I am seeking You with all of my heart. Teach me how to draw nearer to You. Teach me how to "press in" to Your presence.

You have loved me with an everlasting love. Help me to accept Your love. You have a plan for my life, and it's better than the one I'm living.

I have only this lifetime to prepare for eternity. I realize my choices can have eternal consequences. Please cause me to make the right choices. Teach me to do Your will. Reveal to me the path I should walk to find joy in Your presence. Cause me to seek You earnestly. Cause me to trust in Your Word.

Psalm 63:1–4, NIV

O God, you are my God, earnestly I seek you; my soul thirsts for you . . . I have seen you in the sanctuary and beheld your power and your glory. Because your love is better than life, my lips will glorify you. I will praise you as long as I live.

Jeremiah 31:3, NKJV

The LORD has appeared of old to me, saying: "Yes, I have loved you with an everlasting love; therefore with lovingkindness I have drawn you."

Jeremiah 29:11–14, NIV

"I know the plans I have for you," declares the LORD, "plans to prosper you and not to harm you, plans to give you hope and a future. Then you will call upon me and come and pray to me, and I will listen to you. You will seek me and find me when you seek me with all your heart. I will be found by you," declares the LORD, "and will bring you back from captivity."

Deuteronomy 30:19, 20, NKJV

"I have set before you life and death, blessing and cursing; therefore choose life . . . that you may love the LORD your God, that you may obey His voice, and that you may cling to Him, for He is your life."

Psalm 143:10, AMP

Teach me to do Your will, for You are my God; let Your good Spirit lead me into a level country and into the land of uprightness.

Psalm 16:11, NKJV

You will show me the path of life; in Your presence is fullness of joy; at Your right hand are pleasures forevermore.

53. God Is My Teacher

I trust in the Lord with all my heart. I am confident of His love for me and of His goodness toward me. I am confident of His wisdom and His power. I seek His divine guidance in everything I do and say. My desire is to do His will. I acknowledge Him in all my ways—making certain I do not ignore His instructions.

He teaches me what is best for me and directs my path. He keeps watch over me—His eye is constantly upon me. He tells me the way in which I should go, directing me to a good life in this present time and to eternal life with Him in the future.

Proverbs 3:5, 6, AMP

Lean on, trust in, and be confident in the Lord with all your heart and mind and do not rely on your own insight or understanding. In all your ways know, recognize, and acknowledge Him, and He will direct and make straight and plain your paths.

John 14:26, NASB

"The Helper, the Holy Spirit, whom the Father will send in My name, He will teach you all things, and bring to your remembrance all that I said to you."

Luke 12:12, NASB

"For the Holy Spirit will teach you in that very hour what you ought to say."

Isaiah 48:17, NKJV

"I am the LORD your God, who teaches you to profit, who leads you by the way you should go."

Psalm 32:8, 9, AMP

I [the Lord] will instruct you and teach you in the way you should go; I will counsel you with My eye upon you. Be not like the horse or the mule, which lack understanding, which must have their mouths held firm with bit and bridle, or else they will not come with you.

Isaiah 30:20, 21, NASB

Although the Lord has given you bread of privation and water of oppression, He, your Teacher will no longer hide Himself, but your eyes will behold your Teacher. Your ears will hear a word behind you, "This is the way, walk in it," whenever you turn to the right or to the left.

54. God Knows the End From the Beginning

God knows the end from the beginning. The purpose, plan, and works of God (those things He predestined to accomplish) came into existence at the foundation of the world. God never ceases His divine work. He works out everything in harmony with His purpose, according to His plan. I am part of His plan. He determined to adopt me when I accepted Christ. He made me accepted in the Beloved and prepared me an inheritance.

He calls things that are not as though they already were—He regards His Word and His promises that He has yet to reveal by physical evidence, as though they already existed and proclaims them accomplished in Christ. I can too!

Isaiah 46:10, NIV

"I make known the end from the beginning, from ancient times, what is still to come."

Hebrews 4:3, NKJV

The works were finished from the foundation of the world.

John 5:17, AMP

Jesus answered them, My Father has worked [even] until now, [He has never ceased working; He is still working] and I, too, must be at [divine] work.

Ephesians 1:4–7, NKJV

Just as He chose us in Him before the foundation of the world, that we should be holy and without blame before Him in love, having predestined us to adoption as sons by Jesus Christ to Himself, according to the good pleasure of His will . . . by which He has made us accepted in the Beloved. In Him we have redemption through His blood, the forgiveness of sins, according to the riches of His grace.

Ephesians 1:11, NKJV

In whom also we have obtained an inheritance, being predestined according to the purpose of Him who works all things according to the counsel of His will.

Romans 4:17, NIV

The God who gives life to the dead and calls things that are not as though they were.

Romans 4:17, NKJV

God, who gives life to the dead and calls those things which do not exist as though they did.

55. God Knows Me Intimately

Lord, I am poor and needy and—yet—You think on me. I am significant to You. Your eyes were upon me before my birth. Because You know the end from the beginning, all the days of my life were recorded in Your book before they came into being. Your thoughts toward me are precious.

You know me intimately, Father. You know my wanderings. You have a record of my tears and my conversations about You. You know my thoughts and what I'm about to say. Nothing I do surprises You. Even the very hairs on my head are numbered by You.

Lord, You will not forget me—I am inscribed on the palms of Your hands. Thank You, Father, for Your thoughts and plans toward me. I know they are all for my eternal benefit.

Psalm 40:17, NKJV

I am poor and needy; yet the Lord thinks upon me.

Psalm 139:13–17, AMP

Your eyes saw my unformed substance, and in Your book all the days [of my life] were written before ever they took shape, when as yet there was none of them. How precious and weighty also are Your thoughts to me, O God! How vast is the sum of them!

Psalm 139:1–4, AMP

O Lord, you have searched me [thoroughly] and have known me. You know my downsitting and my uprising; You understand my thought afar off. You sift and search out my path and my lying down, and You are acquainted with all my ways. For there is not a word in my tongue [still unuttered], but, behold, O Lord, You know it altogether.

Malachi 3:16, NKJV

Those who feared the Lord spoke to one another, and the Lord listened and heard them; so a book of remembrance was written before Him for those who fear the Lord and who meditate on His name.

Psalm 56:8, NKJV

You number my wanderings; put my tears into Your bottle; are they not in Your book?

Luke 12:7, NKJV

"The very hairs of your head are all numbered."

Isaiah 49:15, 16, NKJV

"I will not forget you. See, I have inscribed you on the palms of My Hands."

56. God Will Meet All Your Needs

I conduct myself in a manner pleasing to God, and He gives me all good things. I don't worry about my needs. I seek first His kingdom and His righteousness, and He maintains my cause—providing as each day may require. I am quick to share my blessings, for with the measure of giving I apply, God measures it back to me. I sow bountifully, and He gives me an abundance for every good work. He supplies all my needs according to His glorious riches in Christ Jesus.

Psalm 84:11, NASB

The Lord God is a sun and shield; the Lord gives grace and glory; no good thing does He withhold from those who walk uprightly.

James 1:17, NIV

Every good and perfect gift is from above, coming down from the Father of the heavenly lights, who does not change like shifting shadows.

Matthew 6:25, 32, 33, NASB

"For this reason I say to you, do not be worried about your life, as to what you will eat or what you will drink; nor for your body, as to what you will put on. Is not life more than food, and the body more than clothing? . . . Your heavenly Father knows that you need all these things. But seek first His kingdom and His righteousness, and all these things will be added to you."

1 Kings 8:59, NKJV

"May these words of mine, with which I have made supplication . . . be near the Lord our God day and night, that He may maintain the cause of His servant . . . as each day may require."

Luke 6:38, NKJV

"Give, and it will be given to you: good measure, pressed down, shaken together, and running over will be put into your bosom. For with the same measure that you use, it will be measured back to you."

Philippians 4:19, NASB

My God will supply all your needs according to His riches in glory in Christ Jesus.

57. God's Presence Is With Me

My Lord is with me at every moment and every step of the way. He never leaves me. He never forsakes me. I know and listen to His voice. God impresses His thoughts upon my mind. The still small voice of the Lord (see 1 Kings 19:12) instructs me in the way I should go. I will not follow the voice of a stranger. I acknowledge His constant presence with me. In His presence, I find fullness of joy and set my heart at rest.

Hebrews 13:5, 6, NIV

Be content with what you have, because God has said, **"Never will I leave you; never will I forsake you."** So we say with confidence, "The Lord is my helper; I will not be afraid. What can man do to me?"

John 10:14, 15, NIV

"I am the good shepherd; I know my sheep and my sheep know me—just as the Father knows me and I know the Father."

John 10:27, AMP

The sheep that are My own hear and are listening to My voice; and I know them, and they follow Me.

Isaiah 30:20, 21, NASB

He, your Teacher will no longer hide Himself, but your eyes will behold your Teacher. Your ears will hear a word behind you, "This is the way, walk in it," whenever you turn to the right or to the left.

John 10:3–5, NIV

"He calls his own sheep by name and leads them out. When he has brought out all his own, he goes on ahead of them, and his sheep follow him because they know his voice. But **they will never follow a stranger;** in fact, they will run away from him because they do not recognize a stranger's voice."

Psalm 16:11, NKJV

You will show me the path of life; in Your presence is fullness of joy; at Your right hand are pleasures forevermore.

1 John 3:19, NIV

This then is how we know that we belong to the truth, and how we set our hearts at rest in his presence.

58. God's Will—My Sanctification

Holy and righteous Father, thank You for giving me the mind of Christ through Your Word and by the power of Your Spirit, Who gives me spiritual understanding and discernment. Just as Jesus did nothing of His own initiative, but sought to do Your will, so do I.

Cause my mind to be renewed by Your Word and fill me with knowledge of You that I might walk worthy of Your calling. Teach me, Lord, to do what is pleasing in Your sight and lead me by Your Spirit. Thank You for equipping me in every good thing to do Your will!

I know my sanctification is Your will for my life. You desire for me to be made holy, set apart for Your good purposes. Oh, Lord, bless me in obeying Your Word. You have entrusted me with the knowledge of Your will, as found written in the Bible. I am required to prove myself faithful in practicing it. I delight to do Your will, Father.

1 Corinthians 2:14–16, NIV

The man without the Spirit does not accept the things that come from the Spirit of God, for they are foolishness to him, and he cannot understand them, because they are spiritually discerned. . . . But we have the mind of Christ.

John 5:30, NASB

"I can do nothing on My own initiative. As I hear, I judge; and My judgment is just, because I do not seek My own will, but the will of Him who sent Me."

Romans 12:2, NASB

Do not be conformed to this world, but be transformed by the renewing of your mind, so that you may prove what the will of God is, that which is good and acceptable and perfect.

Colossians 1:9, 10, NKJV

Ask that you may be filled with the knowledge of His will in all wisdom and spiritual understanding; that you may walk worthy of the Lord, fully pleasing Him, being fruitful in every good work and increasing in the knowledge of God.

Psalm 143:10, NIV

Teach me to do your will, for you are my God; may your good Spirit lead me on level ground.

Hebrews 13:20, 21, NASB

May the God of peace . . . equip you in every good thing to do His will, working in us that which is pleasing in His sight, through Jesus Christ.

1 Thessalonians 4:3, NASB

This is the will of God, your sanctification.

Luke 11:28, AMP

But He said, Blessed . . . rather are those who **hear** the Word of God and **obey** and **practice** it!

1 Corinthians 4:2, NIV

Now it is required that those who have been given a trust must prove faithful.

Psalm 40:8, NASB

"I delight to do Your will, O my God; Your Law is within my heart."

59. God's Word—the Power to Transform

My Father, I stand in awe of the creative and transforming power of Your Word! I praise You for making Your Word alive and active within me—renewing and revitalizing my life.

I trust Your precious promises are for me. As I apply them to my life and put Your Word into daily practice, I thank You for releasing Your power in me—causing me to become a partaker of Your divine nature. By applying Your promises, I escape the devil's clutches.

Thank You for sustaining me by Your mighty Word of power. Cause me to have a more intimate relationship with the Bible, that I might have a more intimate relationship with You.

Hebrews 4:12, NASB

The word of God is living and active and sharper than any two-edged sword, and piercing as far as the division of soul and spirit, of both joints and marrow, and able to judge the thoughts and intentions of the heart.

1 Thessalonians 2:13, NASB

For this reason we also constantly thank God that when you received the word of God which you heard from us, you accepted it not as the word of men, but for what it really is, the word of God, which also performs its work in you who believe.

2 Peter 1:4, NKJV

By which have been given to us exceedingly great and precious promises, that through these you may be partakers of the divine nature, having escaped the corruption that is in the world through lust.

Hebrews 1:3, AMP

He is the sole expression of the glory of God . . . , and He is the perfect imprint and very image of [God's] nature, upholding and maintaining and guiding and propelling the universe by His mighty word of power.

John 8:31, 32, NKJV

Then Jesus said to those Jews who believed Him, "If you abide in My word, you are My disciples indeed. And you shall know the truth, and the truth shall make you free."

60. Grace, Alone and Always

I am what I am by the grace of God! Everything concerning God's kingdom comes to me by grace. Grace is the unearned, undeserved gifts of God. His greatest gifts are Christ in me—my hope of glory, the Holy Spirit, and His written Word. These gifts make grace more than merely unmerited favor. Grace is the force of divine assistance working within me—God's supernatural power for salvation!

By His grace, and through my faith in Him, I have been given the gift of salvation. His grace empowers me to obey as Jesus obeyed and secures my eternal salvation. I am sanctified by grace to obey by grace, as God works in me to will and to act according to His good pleasure.

Saved by God's mercy, I am justified by grace. My works evidence my justification, just as the works of Abraham and Rahab deemed them to be in right standing with God. I am made righteous by grace to practice righteousness by grace.

By His grace—His supernatural power for salvation working in my life—God will complete the good work He has begun in me. I am what I am by His grace, alone and always!

1 Corinthians 15:10, NASB

By the grace of God I am what I am, and His grace toward me did not prove vain; but I labored even more than all of them, yet not I, but the grace of God with me.

Ephesians 2:8–10, NASB

By grace you have been saved through faith; and that not of yourselves, it is the gift of God; not as a result of works, so that no one may boast. For we are His workmanship, created in Christ Jesus for good works, which God prepared beforehand so that we would walk in them.

Hebrews 5:8, 9, NKJV

Though He [Jesus] was a Son, yet He learned obedience by the things which He suffered. And having been perfected, He became the author of eternal salvation to all who obey Him.

1 Thessalonians 5:23, 24, NASB

May the God of peace Himself sanctify you entirely; and may your spirit and soul and body be preserved complete, without blame at the coming of our Lord Jesus Christ. Faithful is He who calls you, and He also will bring it to pass.

1 Peter 1:2, AMP

Who were chosen and foreknown by God the Father and consecrated (sanctified, made holy) by the Spirit to be obedient to Jesus Christ (the Messiah).

Philippians 2:13, NKJV

It is God who works in you both to will and to do for His good pleasure.

Titus 3:5–7, NASB

He saved us, not on the basis of deeds which we have done in righteousness, but according to His mercy, by the washing of regeneration and renewing by the Holy Spirit, whom He poured out upon us richly through Jesus Christ our Savior, so that being justified by His grace we would be made heirs according to the hope of eternal life.

James 2:22–26, NKJV

Do you see that faith was working together with his works, and by works faith was made perfect? And the Scripture was fulfilled which says, "Abraham believed God, and it was accounted to him for righteousness." And he was called the friend of God. You see then that a man is justified by works, and not by faith only. Likewise, was not Rahab the harlot also justified by works when she received the messengers and sent them out another way? For as the body without the spirit is dead, so faith without works is dead also.

2 Corinthians 5:21, NASB

He made Him who knew no sin to be sin on our behalf, so that we might become the righteousness of God in Him.

1 John 3:7, 8, NKJV

Little children, let no one deceive you. He who practices righteousness is righteous, just as He is righteous. He who sins is of the devil, for the devil has sinned from the beginning. For this purpose the Son of God was manifested, that He might destroy the works of the devil.

Philippians 1:6, NKJV

He who has begun a good work in you will complete it until the day of Jesus Christ.

61. Grafted Into the Vine

Jesus is the vine. I am grafted into Him and share in the nourishing sap of His root. His sap—the Spirit's anointing power—works in me to produce love, joy, and peace that I experience within; patience, kindness, and goodness that I express toward humankind; faithfulness, humility, and self-control that I demonstrate toward God. I bear fruit that is good, righteous, and filled with sweet truth.

From time to time, God takes me through a much-needed pruning process. It can be painful, but the precious result is that I bear more fruit. I continue in His goodness; I will not be cut off. I bear fruit in every good work as He strengthens me with all of His power. I will bear fruit in my old age. Jesus, my Vine, will keep me spiritually fresh and flourishing always.

John 15:5, NASB

"I am the vine, you are the branches; he who abides in Me and I in him, he bears much fruit, for apart from Me you can do nothing."

Romans 11:17, NIV

Some of the branches have been broken off, and you, though a wild olive shoot, have been grafted in among the others and now share in the nourishing sap from the olive root.

Galatians 5:22, 23, AMP

The fruit of the [Holy] Spirit [the work which His presence within accomplishes] is love, joy (gladness), peace, patience (an even temper, forbearance), kindness, goodness (benevolence), faithfulness, gentleness (meekness, humility), self-control (self-restraint, continence).

John 15:2, NKJV

"Every branch in Me that does not bear fruit He takes away; and every branch that bears fruit He prunes, that it may bear more fruit."

Romans 11:21–23, NKJV

If God did not spare the natural branches, He may not spare you either. Therefore consider the goodness and severity of God: on those who fell, severity; but toward you, goodness, if you continue in His goodness. Otherwise you also will be cut off. And they also, if they do not continue in unbelief, will be grafted in, for God is able to graft them in again.

Psalm 92:14, NKJV

They shall still bear fruit in old age; they shall be fresh and flourishing.

62. Greater Is He Who Is in Me

Greater is Jesus (who abides in my heart) and His Holy Spirit (who indwells me) than any demonic force on earth. At Calvary's cross, Christ triumphed over Satan and his unholy alliance by making a public spectacle of them and stripping them of their power and authority.

Christ's power and strength are made perfect in my weakness. I acknowledge the weakness of "self." I gladly lay down my limited human power and depend on the unlimited power of His Holy Spirit.

Father, I hunger and thirst for holiness. Please fill me with Your Spirit continuously! Cause me to understand my total dependence upon You. Please fill me with knowledge of Your will, spiritual wisdom, and understanding, that I may conduct my life in a manner worthy of You. Please strengthen me with all power, according to Your glorious might.

1 John 4:4, NASB

Greater is He who is in you than he who is in the world.

Colossians 2:15, NIV

Having disarmed the powers and authorities, he made a public spectacle of them, triumphing over them by the cross.

2 Corinthians 12:9, NIV

He said to me, "My grace is sufficient for you, for my power is made perfect in weakness."

Ephesians 3:16, AMP

May He grant you out of the rich treasure of His glory to be **strengthened** and reinforced **with mighty power** in the inner man by the [Holy] Spirit [Himself indwelling your innermost being and personality].

Matthew 5:6, NKJV

"Blessed are those who hunger and thirst for righteousness, for they shall be filled."

Colossians 1:9–11, NASB

Ask that you may be filled with the knowledge of His will in all spiritual wisdom and understanding, so that you will walk in a manner worthy of the Lord, to please Him in all respects, bearing fruit in every good work and increasing in the knowledge of God; strengthened with all power, according to His glorious might.

63. Guard the Ears—the Standard of Truth Is the Bible

I guard my ears. The only message I receive as truth comes from the Word of God. God has awakened my ears to hear as a disciple taught by the Lord.

Faith comes by hearing. Speaking His Word aloud will increase my faith as I listen to my own voice. Without faith, I cannot please my heavenly Father. God's promises are ushered into existence by faith.

I believe what God has said and testify He is truthful. The message I hear benefits me, because I blend it with actions of faith.

Mark 4:24, AMP

He said to them, **Be careful what you are hearing.** The measure [of thought and study] you give [to the truth you hear] will be the measure [of virtue and knowledge] that comes back to you—and more [besides] will be given to you who hear.

Isaiah 50:5, 4, AMP

The Lord God has opened My ear, and I have not been rebellious or turned backward. He wakens my ear to hear as a disciple [as one who is taught].

Romans 10:17, NIV

Faith comes from hearing the message, and the message is heard through the word of Christ.

Hebrews 11:1, AMP

Faith is the assurance (the confirmation, the title deed) of the things [we] hope for, being the proof of things [we] do not see and the conviction of their reality [faith perceiving as real fact what is not revealed to the senses].

1 John 5:10, NIV

Anyone who does not believe God has made him out to be a liar.

Hebrews 11:6, NIV

Without faith it is impossible to please God, because anyone who comes to him must believe that he exists and that he rewards those who earnestly seek him.

Hebrews 4:2, AMP

For indeed we have had the glad tidings [Gospel of God] proclaimed to us just as truly as they [the Israelites of old did . . .]; **but the message they heard did not benefit them, because it was not mixed with faith . . . by those who heard it.**

64. Guard the Eyes—Keep Them Focused on Jesus

I guard my eyes. I keep my eyes focused on Jesus beholding His love, light, life, and power. I become what I behold. Developing His character is the ultimate plan for my life. I behold His righteousness and will be happy when I become like Him.

I turn my eyes away from worthless things. I have made a covenant with my eyes not to lust and look upon evil.

Oh Lord, my God, cause me to look upon all people and all situations from Your perspective and not from my human viewpoint. Cause my spiritual eyes to look upon the heart of a person, and not what they appear to be outwardly.

Anoint my eyes with Your eye salve, that I may see as You see.

Hebrews 12:2, NIV

Let us fix our eyes on Jesus, the author and perfecter of our faith.

2 Corinthians 3:18, NKJV

We all, with unveiled face, beholding as in a mirror the glory of the Lord, are being transformed into the same image from glory to glory, just as by the Spirit of the Lord.

Psalm 17:15, KJV

As for me, I will behold thy face in righteousness: I shall be satisfied, when I awake, with thy likeness.

Psalm 119:37, NIV

Turn my eyes away from worthless things; preserve my life according to your word.

Job 31:1, NIV

"I made a covenant with my eyes not to look lustfully at a girl."

2 Corinthians 5:16, AMP

From now on we . . . regard no one from a [purely] human point of view.

1 Samuel 16:7, NKJV

But the LORD said to Samuel, "Do not look at his appearance or at his physical stature, because I have refused him. For the LORD does not see as man sees; for man looks at the outward appearance, but the LORD looks at the heart."

Revelation 3:18, NKJV

"Anoint your eyes with eye salve, that you may see."

65. Guard the Heart—I Am Who God Says I Am

I guard my heart, for as I think in my heart, so shall I become.
I am who God says I am. I am destined to become like Jesus.
God places life-and-death choices before me daily. I choose to believe the faithfulness of His Word and by doing so **I choose life,** for His Word preserves my life.
I walk in perfect peace, because I trust the Lord and keep my mind focused on His faithfulness. The goodness of God is stored in my heart and overflows to my mouth. From my heart, I think and speak only that which is pleasing to my heavenly Father.

Proverbs 4:20–23, NIV

Pay attention to what I say; listen closely to my words. Do not let them out of your sight, keep them within your heart; **for they are life to those who find them** and health to a man's whole body. Above all else, **guard your heart,** for it is the wellspring of life.

Proverbs 23:7, AMP

As he thinks in his heart, so is he.

1 Corinthians 15:10, NASB

By the grace of God I am what I am, and His grace toward me did not prove vain.

Romans 8:28, 29, NKJV

And we know that all things work together for good to those who love God, to those who are the called according to His purpose. For whom He foreknew, He also predestined to be conformed to the image of His Son.

Deuteronomy 30:19, NKJV

"I call heaven and earth as witnesses today against you, that I have set before you life and death, blessing and cursing; therefore choose life."

Deuteronomy 32:46, 47, NIV

"Take to heart all the words I have solemnly declared to you. . . . They are not just idle words for you—they are your life."

Luke 6:45, NIV

"The good man brings good things out of the good stored up in his heart, and the evil man brings evil things out of the evil stored up in his heart. For out of the overflow of his heart his mouth speaks."

66. Guard the Mouth—the Power of the Tongue

I guard my mouth. The power of life and death is in my tongue.

I believe in my heart, but it is my spoken **confession** of His word that releases His power into my life. I speak in faith—and not in doubt and disbelief. I do not practice ungodliness by speaking faithless error against the Lord. On the day of judgment, I will have to give account of every idle word spoken—every word I uttered that did not line up in agreement with God's Word.

His Word is in my mouth and in my heart. I confess the word of faith over my life without wavering, for He Who promised is faithful. I speak God's Word over my life and know that He is watching to perform it. By that same spirit of faith and with the tongue of an instructed disciple, I speak His counsel to the weary.

Oh, holy and righteous Father, increase my faith in Your faithfulness. Please, loving Lord, don't allow me to doubt Your promises. Cause me to believe—because I keep Your commandments and do what is pleasing in Your sight—that I receive what You have faithfully promised. Help me to understand that whatever I ask in agreement with Your Word will be done, as Jesus promised. To my limited human understanding, this sounds too good to be true. Cause me to know this is faith—not presumption.

Proverbs 21:23, NKJV

Whoever guards his mouth and tongue keeps his soul from troubles.

Psalm 141:3, NKJV

Set a guard, O LORD, over my mouth; keep watch over the door of my lips.

Proverbs 18:21, NIV

The tongue has the **power of life and death** and those who love it will eat its fruit.

Isaiah 32:6, NASB

A fool speaks nonsense, and his heart inclines toward wickedness: to practice ungodliness and to **speak error** against the LORD.

Matthew 12:36, 37, AMP

I tell you, on the day of judgment men will have to **give account for every idle (inoperative, nonworking) word they speak.** For by your words you will be justified and acquitted, and by your words you will be condemned and sentenced.

Romans 10:8–10, NIV

"The word is near you; it is in your mouth and in your heart," that is, the **word of faith** we are proclaiming: That if you confess with your mouth, "Jesus is Lord," and believe in your heart that God raised Him from the dead, you will be saved. For it is with your heart that you believe and are justified, and it is with your **mouth** that you **confess and are saved.**

Hebrews 10:23, NKJV

Let us hold fast the **confession of our hope** without wavering, for He who promised is faithful.

2 Corinthians 4:13, NIV

It is written: "I believed; therefore I have spoken." With that same **spirit of faith** we also believe and therefore speak.

Jeremiah 1:12, AMP

Then said the Lord to me, You have seen well, for I am alert and active, watching over My word to perform it.

Isaiah 50:4, AMP

The Lord God has given Me the tongue of a disciple and of one who is taught, that I should know how to speak a word in season to him who is weary.

Mark 11:22–24, NKJV

So Jesus answered . . . "Have faith in God. For assuredly, I say to you, whoever says . . . and does not doubt in his heart, but believes that those things he says will come to pass, he will have whatever he says. Therefore I say to you, whatever things you ask when you pray, believe that you receive them, and you will have them."

1 John 3:22, NKJV

Whatever we ask we receive from Him, because we keep His commandments and do those things that are pleasing in His sight.

1 John 5:14, 15, NASB

This is the confidence which we have before Him, that, if we ask anything according to His will, He hears us. And if we know that He hears us in whatever we ask, we know that we have the requests which we have asked from Him.

67. Hardships—Blessings in Disguise

The hardships I've suffered and the times of tremendous pressure which have brought me to despair, my Lord has **allowed** to happen, so I will learn not to rely on myself, but rather to rely on Him. He is my deliverer and on Him I set my hope. He will continue to deliver me through His gracious favor, granted in answer to my earnest prayers.

I know the testing of my faith develops perseverance that is doing a good work in me. No matter how difficult my circumstances, I will not allow the devil to tempt me to doubt God's love and His promises. God will provide the way out of this temptation. I will not allow unbelief to shut me out of His rest. By the power of the Holy Spirit, I am bubbling over with hope. God fills me with all joy and peace as I continue to trust in Him.

2 Corinthians 1:8, 9, NIV

We do not want you to be uninformed . . . about the hardships we suffered. . . . We were under great pressure, far beyond our ability to endure, so that we despaired even of life. Indeed, in our hearts we felt the sentence of death. **But this happened that we might not rely on ourselves but on God**.

James 1:2–4, NIV

Consider it pure joy, my brothers, whenever you face trials of many kinds, because you know that the testing of your faith develops perseverance. Perseverance must finish its work so that you may be mature and complete, not lacking anything.

1 Corinthians 10:13, NASB

No temptation has overtaken you but such as is common to man; and God is faithful, who will not allow you to be tempted beyond what you are able, but with the temptation will provide the way of escape also, so that you will be able to endure it.

Hebrews 3:18, 19, AMP

To whom did He swear that they should not enter His rest, but to those who disobeyed [who had not listened to His word and who refused to be compliant or be persuaded]? So we see that they were not able to enter [into His rest], because of their unwillingness to adhere to and trust in and rely on God [unbelief had shut them out].

Romans 15:13, NKJV

Now may the God of hope fill you with all joy and peace in believing, that you may abound in hope by the power of the Holy Spirit.

68. Health Given by God

It is the name of Jesus Christ (representing all He is) and the faith that comes through Him that gives me complete healing. I follow God's instructions for health and healing. The Lord, Jehovah-rapha, is my Counselor and healer. By His grace, I am walking in God-given health (spiritual, mental, emotional, and physical health). I trust God to give me the healing that He knows I need. He has my eternal benefit in mind. He took up my infirmities and carried all my diseases. He sent His Living Word, Jesus Christ, Who was bruised for my iniquities. By His stripes I was healed!

Acts 3:16, NIV

"By faith in the name of Jesus, this man whom you see and know was made strong. It is Jesus' name and the faith that comes through him that has given this complete healing to him, as you can all see."

Exodus 15:26, NKJV

"If you diligently heed the voice of the LORD your God and do what is right in His sight, give ear to His commandments and keep all His statutes, I will put none of the diseases on you which I have brought on the Egyptians. For I am the LORD who heals you."

Psalm 103:2, 3, NKJV

Bless the LORD, O my soul, and forget not all His benefits: Who forgives all your iniquities, Who heals all your diseases.

Matthew 8:16, 17, AMP

When evening came, they brought to Him many who were under the power of demons, and He drove out the spirits with a word and restored to health all who were sick. And thus He fulfilled what was spoken by the prophet Isaiah, He Himself took [in order to carry away] our weaknesses and infirmities and bore away our diseases.

Psalm 107:20, AMP

He sends forth His word and heals them.

Isaiah 53:4, 5, NIV

Surely he took up our infirmities and carried our sorrows. . . . The punishment that brought us peace was upon him, and by his wounds we are healed.

1 Peter 2:24, NKJV

By whose stripes you were healed.

69. Hedge of Protection

I am hedged in by God's grace. He surrounds me with loving-kindness. He is a wall of fire around me and the glory in my midst. He watches over me continuously and keeps me from all harm. I am blessed with His hedge of protection. God goes before me and behind me (serving as my rear guard). His truth and His faithfulness are my shield and buckler. I dwell in the secret place of the Most High, and in Him I put my trust. He is my deliverer.

Psalm 5:12, NKJV

For You, O LORD, will bless the righteous; with favor You will surround him as with a shield.

Zechariah 2:5, NASB

" 'For I,' declares the Lord, 'will be a wall of fire around her, and I will be the glory in her midst.' "

Psalm 121:1–8, NIV

I lift up my eyes to the hills—where does my help come from? My help comes from the LORD, the Maker of heaven and earth. He will not let your foot slip—he who watches over you will not slumber; indeed, he who watches over Israel will neither slumber nor sleep. The LORD watches over you . . . The LORD will keep you from all harm—he will watch over your life; the LORD will watch over your coming and going both now and forevermore.

Job 1:10, NKJV

"Have You not made a hedge around him, around his household, and around all that he has on every side?"

Isaiah 52:12, NKJV

The LORD will go before you, and the God of Israel will be your rear guard.

Psalm 91:1–4, AMP

He who dwells in the secret place of the Most High shall remain stable and fixed under the shadow of the Almighty [Whose power no foe can withstand]. I will say of the Lord, He is my Refuge and my Fortress, my God; on Him I lean and rely, and in Him I [confidently] trust! For [then] He will deliver you from the snare of the fowler and from the deadly pestilence. [Then] He will cover you with His pinions, and under His wings shall you trust and find refuge; His truth and His faithfulness are a shield and a buckler.

70. Help, Lord!

Help, Lord! I don't understand this situation, and I really don't know how I should pray. All I can say is please help me, Father! What a relief it is to know that the Holy Spirit is interceding for me right now. Thank You for hearing His prayer. And how glad I am to know that You, Lord Jesus, are interceding on my behalf. I know You are able to save me completely.

Thank You, Father, for hearing and answering. I will not be fearful, for I am confident You will provide a solution. I count on Your help! You will strengthen me and uphold me with Your righteous right hand. I will keep my mind fixed on You, trusting in You. Thank You for perfect peace—that is above human understanding. I will not be anxious about anything, because Your peace guards my heart and mind in Christ Jesus.

Psalm 12:1, NKJV

Help, Lord . . . !

Romans 8:26, 27, NKJV

The Spirit also helps in our weaknesses. For we do not know what we should pray for as we ought, but the Spirit Himself makes intercession for us with groanings which cannot be uttered. Now He who searches the hearts knows what the mind of the Spirit is, because He makes intercession for the saints according to the will of God.

Hebrews 7:25, NKJV

He is also able to save to the uttermost those who come to God through Him, since He always lives to make intercession for them.

Isaiah 41:10, NKJV

" 'Fear not, for I am with you; be not dismayed, for I am your God. I will strengthen you, Yes, I will help you, I will uphold you with My righteous right hand.' "

Isaiah 41:13, NASB

"I am the Lord your God, who upholds your right hand, who says to you, 'Do not fear, I will help you.' "

Philippians 4:6, 7, NIV

Do not be anxious about anything, but in everything, by prayer and petition, with thanksgiving, present your requests to God. And the peace of God, which transcends all understanding, will guard your hearts and your minds in Christ Jesus.

71. The Holy Spirit Abundantly Supplied to Me

I am the living temple of the living God. I am bought with a price too precious to calculate. I am not my own. He saved me through rebirth and renewal of the Holy Spirit, Whom He poured out on me abundantly through Jesus Christ, my Savior.

I am to be filled continually with the Holy Spirit. I give God permission to fill me; I ask and keep on asking for this great gift from above. I walk in obedience. If I keep His commandments, Jesus will ask the Father to send the Helper, the Spirit of truth, to dwell in me. God strengthens me with power through His Spirit. According to that power working within me, He is able to do abundantly beyond what I ask or think.

1 Corinthians 6:19, 20, NKJV

Do you not know that your body is the temple of the Holy Spirit who is in you, whom you have from God, and you are not your own? For you were bought at a price; therefore glorify God in your body and in your spirit, which are God's.

Titus 3:5, 6, NKJV

The Holy Spirit, whom He poured out on us abundantly through Jesus Christ our Savior.

Ephesians 5:18, AMP

Ever be filled and stimulated with the [Holy] Spirit.

Luke 11:9–13, AMP

Ask and keep on asking and it shall be given you. . . . How much more will your heavenly Father give the Holy Spirit to those who ask and continue to ask Him!

John 14:15, 16, NKJV

"If you love Me, keep My commandments. And I will pray the Father, and He will give you another Helper, that He may abide with you forever."

Acts 5:32, NKJV

"The Holy Spirit whom God has given to those who obey Him."

Ephesians 3:16, 20, 21, NASB

That He would grant you, according to the riches of His glory, to be strengthened with power through His Spirit in the inner man . . . Now to Him who is able to do far more abundantly beyond all that we ask or think, according to the power that works within us, to Him be the glory in the church and in Christ Jesus to all generations forever and ever.

72. Hope Bubbling Over

I refuse to allow my circumstances to get me down. My hope is in the Lord. He strengthens my heart and keeps His eye upon me, because I wait for Him and put my hope in His Word. He will fulfill what He has promised; not one word of all He promised will fail. All of His promises are mine as I abide in Christ.

I trust in the Lord with all my heart! I will not lean on my own understanding, but on His Word. I hope for what I do not see, persevering in eager expectation. This hope is the anchor for my soul—keeping me from being double-minded in troublous times. God does not change like shifting shadows. He hears my prayer, and He will answer.

I am blessed because I trust in the Lord and put my hope in Him. I will not fear or be anxious. The God of hope fills me with joy and peace in believing, and by the power of the Holy Spirit, I am bubbling over with hope.

Psalm 42:11, NIV

Why are you downcast, O my soul? Why so disturbed within me? Put your hope in God, for I will yet praise him, my Savior and my God.

Psalm 31:24, NKJV

Be of good courage, and He shall strengthen your heart, all you who hope in the LORD.

Psalm 33:18, AMP

Behold, the Lord's eye is upon those who fear Him [who revere and worship Him with awe], who wait for Him and hope in His mercy and loving-kindness.

Psalm 130:5, NASB

I wait for the LORD, my soul does wait, and in His word do I hope.

Numbers 23:19, NIV

God is not a man, that he should lie, nor a son of man, that he should change his mind. Does he speak and then not act? Does he promise and not fulfill?

1 Kings 8:56, NASB

"Blessed be the LORD . . . according to all that He promised; not one word has failed of all His good promise, which He promised."

2 Corinthians 1:20, NIV

No matter how many promises God has made, they are "Yes" in Christ.

Proverbs 3:5, 6, NKJV

Trust in the Lord with all your heart, and lean not on your own understanding; in all your ways acknowledge Him, and He shall direct your paths.

Romans 8:24, 25, NKJV

For we were saved in this hope, but hope that is seen is not hope; for why does one still hope for what he sees? But if we hope for what we do not see, then we eagerly wait for it with perseverance.

Hebrews 6:19, NKJV

This hope we have as an anchor of the soul, both sure and steadfast.

James 1:6–8, NKJV

But let him ask in faith, with no doubting, for he who doubts is like a wave of the sea driven and tossed by the wind. For let not that man suppose that he will receive anything from the Lord; he is a double-minded man, unstable in all his ways.

James 1:17, NIV

Every good and perfect gift is from above, coming down from the Father of the heavenly lights, who does not change like shifting shadows.

Psalm 38:15, NASB

For I hope in You, O Lord; You will answer, O Lord my God.

Jeremiah 17:7, 8, NKJV

"Blessed is the man who trusts in the Lord, and whose hope is the Lord. For he shall be like a tree planted by the waters, which spreads out its roots by the river, and will not fear when heat comes; but its leaf will be green, and will not be anxious in the year of drought, nor will cease from yielding fruit."

Romans 15:13, AMP

May the God of your hope so fill you with all joy and peace in believing [through the experience of your faith] that by the power of the Holy Spirit you may abound and be overflowing (bubbling over) with hope.

73. How Much More Will He Freely Give?

God is the giver of every good and perfect gift—evidenced by His glorious gift of salvation! How much more will He freely give? My salvation is not according to any works of righteousness that I have done, but by the grace of God. He demonstrated His love for me by sending Jesus as the perfect sacrifice for my sins.

I am saved through the washing of rebirth and renewing of the Holy Spirit. I am filled by the Holy Spirit, whom God poured out on me abundantly through Jesus Christ my Savior. I am justified by His grace—He counts me as being conformed to His divine will—that I might become an heir of eternal life according to my hope.

Father, if You sent Jesus to die for me while I was yet a sinner, how much more will You now freely give me all that You have promised? All of Your promises are mine now that I am in Christ. Help me always to remember that You are the giver of every good and perfect gift. As the perfect Father, you lavish Your love on me, Your child.

Titus 3:4–7, NKJV

But when the kindness and the love of God our Savior toward man appeared, not by works of righteousness which we have done, but according to His mercy He saved us, through the washing of regeneration and renewing of the Holy Spirit, whom He poured out on us abundantly through Jesus Christ our Savior, that having been justified by His grace we should become heirs according to the hope of eternal life.

Romans 5:8, NASB

God demonstrates His own love toward us, in that while we were yet sinners, Christ died for us.

Romans 8:31, 32, NKJV

What then shall we say to these things? If God is for us, who can be against us? He who did not spare His own Son, but delivered Him up for us all, how shall He not with Him also freely give us all things?

2 Corinthians 1:20, NIV

No matter how many promises God has made, they are "Yes" in Christ. And so through him the "Amen" is spoken by us to the glory of God.

James 1:17, NIV

Every good and perfect gift is from above, coming down from the Father of the heavenly lights, who does not change like shifting shadows.

74. Humility Comes Before Honor

I know humility comes before honor, so I humble myself before the Lord. I treasure the day of small beginnings. If I am faithful with regard to small things, God will trust me with more. God will exalt me in His perfect timing.

Father, by Your grace, I will be clothed with humility—humbling myself under Your mighty hand. Thank You, Father, for making Jesus Christ my wisdom from You. Thank You for the gift of humility that comes from wisdom.

Proverbs 16:18, NIV

Pride goes before destruction, a haughty spirit before a fall.

James 4:10, AMP

Humble yourselves [feeling very insignificant] in the presence of the Lord, and He will exalt you [He will lift you up and make your lives significant].

Zechariah 4:10, AMP

Who [with reason] despises the day of small things?

Luke 16:10, NASB

"He who is faithful in a very little thing is faithful also in much."

1 Peter 5:5–7, NKJV

Yes, all of you be submissive to one another, and be clothed with humility, for "God resists the proud, but gives grace to the humble." Therefore humble yourselves under the mighty hand of God, **that He may exalt you in due time,** casting all your care upon Him, for He cares for you.

James 4:6, AMP

But He gives us more and more grace (power of the Holy Spirit, to meet this evil tendency and all others fully). That is why He says, **God sets Himself against the proud and haughty, but gives grace [continually] to the lowly** (those who are **humble** enough to receive it).

1 Corinthians 1:30, AMP

You have your life in Christ Jesus, Whom God made our Wisdom from God.

Proverbs 11:2, NKJV

When pride comes, then comes shame; but with the humble is wisdom.

75. Intercessory Faithfulness

I am faithful to intercede for others. God has put His compassion in my heart, and He searches to see if I will practice it by standing in the gap for others—lifting them up to Him in prayer. He instructs me to pray for all people—particularly my Christian brothers and sisters. Far be it from me that I should sin against the Lord in ceasing to pray for others. Praying for those who will not pray for themselves gives God permission to intervene in their lives.

I am privileged to participate in intercessory prayer. It is a high calling to ministry. I know this because it is the ministry of my risen and exalted Savior, Who lives to intercede for us.

Ezekiel 22:30, NASB

"I searched for a man among them who would build up the wall and stand in the gap before Me for the land, so that I would not destroy it; but I found no one."

1 Timothy 2:1, 2, NIV

I urge, then, first of all, that requests, prayers, intercession and thanksgiving be made for everyone—for kings and all those in authority, that we may live peaceful and quiet lives in all godliness and holiness.

Ephesians 6:18, AMP

Pray at all times (on every occasion, in every season) in the Spirit, with all [manner of] prayer and entreaty. To that end keep alert and watch with strong purpose and perseverance, interceding in behalf of all the saints (God's consecrated people).

1 Samuel 12:23, NKJV

"Moreover, as for me, far be it from me that I should sin against the Lord in ceasing to pray for you; but I will teach you the good and the right way."

Isaiah 62:6, 7, AMP

I have set watchmen upon your walls, O Jerusalem, who will never hold their peace day or night; you who [are His servants and by your prayers] put the Lord in remembrance [of His promises], keep not silence, and give Him no rest until He establishes Jerusalem and makes her a praise in the earth.

Hebrews 7:25, NKJV

Therefore He is also able to save to the uttermost those who come to God through Him, since He always lives to make intercession for them.

76. Joy Comes in the Morning

Jesus came to heal my broken heart, to set me free from sin, to comfort and console me. He renews my thoughts. To replace the ashes of mourning, He fills my cup with the oil of joy. To replace the spirit of heaviness, He offers me the garment of praise. He shines His light into the recesses of my mind and illuminates my darkness.

I choose to follow His command to arise from the depression of my circumstances. By His grace, I will shine in spite of my situation. Though it might appear that all of my efforts have yielded nothing fruitful, I will find joy in the God of my salvation. He is my strength. He makes me as sure-footed as a deer and gives my trembling legs the strength to go forward on my high places. I will brace up my faltering knees and make straight paths for my feet, so that I will be healed. I will sing praises to Him—His favor is forever.

Weeping may endure for a night, but joy comes in the morning!

Isaiah 61:1–3, NKJV

"He has sent Me to heal the brokenhearted, to proclaim liberty to the captives, and the opening of the prison to those who are bound; to proclaim the acceptable year of the LORD, and the day of vengeance of our God; to comfort all who mourn . . . to give them beauty for ashes, the oil of joy for mourning, the garment of praise for the spirit of heaviness."

2 Samuel 22:29, AMP

For You, O Lord, are my Lamp; the Lord lightens my darkness.

Isaiah 60:1, NASB

"Arise, shine; for your light has come, and the glory of the LORD has risen upon you."

Habakkuk 3:17–19, NASB

Though the fig tree should not blossom and there be no fruit on the vines, though the yield of the olive should fail and the fields produce no food . . . yet I will exult in the LORD, I will rejoice in the God of my salvation. The Lord GOD is my strength, and He has made my feet like hinds' feet, and makes me walk on my high places.

Hebrews 12:12, 13, NASB

Therefore, strengthen the hands that are weak and the knees that are feeble, and make straight paths for your feet, so that the limb which is lame may not be put out of joint, but rather be healed.

Psalm 30:5, AMP

Weeping may endure for a night, but joy comes in the morning.

77. Judge Not, and You Shall Not Be Judged

I am careful not to condemn myself by passing judgment on others, for **everyone** falls short of the glory of God. Judgmental attitudes are the "spirit of self-righteousness." I do not think of myself more highly than I ought to. I don't condemn myself as a hypocrite by picking at the speck of sawdust in my brother's eye while I have a log lodged in my own.

In the brilliance of God's glory and holiness, and in the lap of His abundant grace, there is no room for feelings of spiritual pride or superiority. I gladly replace my **earthly** attitude and mind-set, with the **heavenly** attitude and humble mind of Christ Jesus.

Luke 6:37, NKJV

"Judge not, and you shall not be judged. Condemn not, and you shall not be condemned. Forgive, and you will be forgiven."

Romans 3:23, NIV

All have sinned and fall short of the glory of God

Romans 12:3, NIV

By the grace given me I say to every one of you: **Do not think of yourself more highly than you ought,** but rather think of yourself with sober judgment.

Matthew 7:3–5, NIV

"Why do you look at the speck of sawdust in your brother's eye and pay no attention to the plank in your own eye? How can you say to your brother, 'Let me take the speck out of your eye,' when all the time there is a plank in your own eye? You hypocrite, first take the plank out of your own eye, and then you will see clearly to remove the speck from your brother's eye."

Romans 2:1, 3, NASB

You have no excuse, everyone of you who passes judgment, for in that which you judge another, you condemn yourself; for you who judge practice the same things. . . . But do you suppose this, O man, when you pass judgment on those who practice such things and do the same yourself, that you will escape the judgment of God?

Philippians 2:5, AMP

Let this same attitude and purpose and [humble] mind be in you which was in Christ Jesus: [Let Him be your example in humility].

78. Justified by Grace

Thank You, Father, for washing me by the spiritual water of Your Word. Thank You for washing me—cleansing me of my confessed sins—by the blood of Jesus. Abba, Father, thank You for Your great love and mercy!

I am justified by Your grace, through my faith in Christ Jesus and His complete atonement for my sin. Thank You, Jesus, for being my Savior! Thank You for justifying me—securing my acquittal from guilt, putting me in right standing with God, and releasing me from condemnation. Glory! Glory! Glory!

Ephesians 5:25, 26, NKJV

Christ also loved the church and gave Himself for her, that He might sanctify and cleanse her with the washing of water by the word.

1 John 1:7–9, NKJV

If we walk in the light as He is in the light, we have fellowship with one another, and the blood of Jesus Christ His Son cleanses us from all sin. . . . If we confess our sins, He is faithful and just to forgive us our sins and to cleanse us from all unrighteousness.

Romans 5:1, NASB

Therefore, having been justified by faith, we have peace with God through our Lord Jesus Christ.

1 Corinthians 6:11, AMP

You were washed clean (purified by a complete atonement for sin and made free from the guilt of sin), and you were consecrated (set apart, hallowed), and you were justified [pronounced righteous, by trusting] in the name of the Lord Jesus Christ and in the [Holy] Spirit of our God.

Titus 3:4–7, NKJV

When the kindness and the love of God our Savior toward man appeared, not by works of righteousness which we have done, but according to His mercy He saved us, through the washing of regeneration and renewing of the Holy Spirit, whom He poured out on us abundantly through Jesus Christ our Savior, that having been **justified by His grace** we should become heirs according to the hope of eternal life.

Romans 3:23, 24, NASB

All have sinned and fall short of the glory of God, being justified as a gift by His grace through the redemption which is in Christ Jesus

79. Keep a Finger on Your Spiritual Pulse

I am God-confident—not self-confident. As long as I remain in Christ, I have assurance of salvation. Still I take heed, lest I think I am standing firm when I'm really about to fall.

I keep a finger on my spiritual pulse—checking the time I spend with God in prayer, in the Word, and the practice of His Word. I avoid empty, godless chatter and puffed-up knowledge. I make sure I practice what I preach, so that I will not be disqualified. When I sin, I am zealous to repent.

1 Corinthians 10:12, NKJV

Let him who thinks he stands take heed lest he fall.

2 Corinthians 13:5, NKJV

Examine yourselves as to whether you are in the faith. Test yourselves. Do you not know yourselves, that Jesus Christ is in you?—unless indeed you are disqualified.

James 1:22, NKJV

Be doers of the word, and not hearers only, deceiving yourselves.

James 1:26, NKJV

If anyone among you thinks he is religious, and does not bridle his tongue but deceives his own heart, this one's religion is useless.

2 Timothy 2:16, NIV

Avoid godless chatter, because those who indulge in it will become more and more ungodly.

1 Timothy 6:20, 21, NASB

Guard what has been entrusted to you, avoiding worldly and empty chatter and the opposing arguments of what is falsely called "knowledge"—which some have professed and thus gone astray from the faith.

1 Corinthians 8:1, 2, NKJV

We know that we all have knowledge. Knowledge puffs up, but love edifies. And if anyone thinks that he knows anything, he knows nothing yet as he ought to know.

1 Corinthians 9:27, NIV

I beat my body and make it my slave so that after I have preached to others, I myself will not be disqualified for the prize.

80. Lean Not on Your Own Understanding

My confidence is in the Lord. I trust in Him with all of my heart! I do not lean on my own understanding—I lean on what His Word says.

Human understanding is limited; therefore, human thoughts are futile. God's thoughts and His ways are superior to mine.

I trust in the Lord, and He causes my mind to prosper—He delivers my thoughts from futility. Leaning on God's Word, I walk wisely, understanding and appreciating God's will for my life.

Proverbs 3:5, 6, NKJV

Trust in the LORD with all your heart, and lean not on your own understanding; in all your ways acknowledge Him, and He shall direct your paths.

Proverbs 3:5, AMP

Do not rely on your own insight or understanding.

Psalm 94:11, AMP

The Lord knows the thoughts of man, that they are vain (empty and futile—only a breath).

Isaiah 55:8, 9, NKJV

"My thoughts are not your thoughts, nor are your ways My ways," says the LORD. "For as the heavens are higher than the earth, so are My ways higher than your ways, and My thoughts than your thoughts."

Proverbs 28:25, 26, NASB

He who trusts in the LORD will prosper. He who trusts in his own heart is a fool, but he who walks wisely will be delivered.

Ephesians 5:15–17, NIV

Be very careful, then, how you live—not as unwise but as wise, making the most of every opportunity, because the days are evil. Therefore do not be foolish, but understand what the Lord's will is.

81. The Love of God—I

Heavenly Father, You have loved me and drawn me with Your **everlasting** love. Help me to understand Your heart that overflows with love. I want to grasp how wide and long and high and deep is Your **limitless** love for me. Because of Your **all-inclusive** love, You don't want anyone to perish. That's why You sent Your only begotten Son to give eternal life to all who receive Him.

Loving Father, You demonstrated Your **unearned, undeserved** love by sending Jesus to die for me while I was still a sinner. By Your grace, You made me alive in Christ; salvation is Your gift to me. You re-created me and prepared a good path in which I should walk. Precious Lord, please help me to understand Your love that surpasses human knowledge!

Jeremiah 31:3, NKJV *(Everlasting love)*
"Yes, I have loved you with an everlasting love; therefore with lovingkindness I have drawn you."

Ephesians 3:17–19, NIV *(Limitless love)*
I pray that you, being rooted and established in love, may have power, together with all the saints, to grasp how wide and long and high and deep is the love of Christ, and to know this love that surpasses knowledge.

2 Peter 3:9, NIV *(All-inclusive love)*
The Lord is . . . patient with you, not wanting anyone to perish, but everyone to come to repentance.

John 3:16, NASB *(All-inclusive love)*
For God so loved the world, that He gave His only begotten Son, that whoever believes in Him shall not perish, but have eternal life.

Ephesians 2:4–10, NASB (*Unearned, undeserved love*)
God, being rich in mercy, because of His great love with which He loved us, even when we were dead in our transgressions, made us alive together with Christ (by grace you have been saved). . . . For by grace you have been saved through faith; and that not of yourselves, it is the gift of God; not as a result of works, so that no one may boast. For we are His workmanship, created in Christ Jesus for good works, which God prepared beforehand so that we would walk in them.

82. The Love of God—II

Abba, in **fatherly** love You give me Your name and make me Your child. I know Your fatherly devotion is demonstrated by Your **disciplinary** love. You discipline me for my eternal benefit. Perfect Father, I trust You completely to train me in Your way of righteousness. I pray for Your correction and loving discipline. You love me with a **forgiving** love, blotting out the sins I confess to You. Your love is **protective** over me, for I am precious in Your sight. Your love is **inseparable;** nothing can separate me from Your love. You quiet me with Your love and rejoice over me with singing. Loving Father, please help me to understand Your love that surpasses human knowledge!

1 John 3:1, NKJV *(Fatherly love)*

Behold what manner of love the Father has bestowed on us, that we should be called children of God!

Hebrews 12:6–10, AMP *(Disciplinary love)*

The Lord corrects and disciplines everyone whom He loves. . . . He disciplines us for our certain good, that we may become sharers in His own holiness.

Isaiah 43:25, NKJV *(Forgiving love)*

"I, even I, am He who blots out your transgressions for My own sake; and I will not remember your sins."

1 John 1:9, NKJV *(Forgiving love)*

If we confess our sins, He is faithful and just to forgive us our sins and to cleanse us from all unrighteousness.

Isaiah 43:1–4, NASB *(Protective love)*

"Do not fear, for I have redeemed you; I have called you by name; you are Mine! When you pass through the waters, I will be with you; and through the rivers, they will not overflow you. When you walk through the fire, you will not be scorched, nor will the flame burn you. For I am the LORD your God, the Holy One of Israel, your Savior. . . . Since you are precious in My sight, since you are honored and I love you."

Romans 8:39, NKJV *(Inseparable love)*

[Nothing] shall be able to separate us from the love of God which is in Christ Jesus.

Zephaniah 3:17, NKJV *(Fatherly love)*

He will quiet you with His love, He will rejoice over you with singing.

83. Love the Lord with All Your Heart, Soul, Mind, and Strength

I love the Lord with all my heart, soul, mind, and strength. Even in this response to God, I am totally dependent upon Him.

Father, I know You are the Source of love. Help me to open my heart and allow You to pour Your love into me. Empower me to respond to You in love, and always keep me mindful of Jesus Christ—my First Love.

Mark 12:28–30, NIV

One of the teachers of the law came and heard them debating. Noticing that Jesus had given them a good answer, he asked him, "Of all the commandments, which is the most important?" "The most important one," answered Jesus, "is this: 'Hear, O Israel, the Lord our God, the Lord is one. Love the Lord your God with all your heart and with all your soul and with all your mind and with all your strength.' "

Deuteronomy 30:6, NASB

"Moreover the LORD your God will circumcise your heart and the heart of your descendants, to love the LORD your God with all your heart and with all your soul, so that you may live."

2 Thessalonians 3:5, NKJV

Now may the Lord direct your hearts into the love of God and into the patience of Christ.

1 John 4:16, NASB

We have come to know and have believed the love which God has for us. God is love, and the one who abides in love abides in God, and God abides in him.

Romans 5:5, NKJV

Now hope does not disappoint, because the love of God has been poured out in our hearts by the Holy Spirit who was given to us.

Revelation 2:3–5, NIV

"You have persevered and have endured hardships for my name, and have not grown weary. Yet I hold this against you: You have forsaken your first love. Remember the height from which you have fallen! Repent and do the things you did at first."

84. Love Your Neighbor as Yourself

I live in love, shunning pride and arrogance, despising evil behavior and perverse speech. **I hate the sin**, but **not** the sinner. I love my neighbor as myself, and I am seeking to do good for others—just as I would like to have them do for me.

I realize how much God has forgiven me, which makes my heart swell with love. When it is possible, I demonstrate my love by my actions and not merely by my words. I do not grow weary in my efforts to do good works.

Proverbs 8:13, NIV

> **To fear the LORD is to hate evil**; I hate pride and arrogance, evil behavior and perverse speech.

Mark 12:28–31, NIV

> " 'Love the Lord your God with all your heart and with all your soul and with all your mind and with all your strength . . . Love your neighbor as yourself.' There is no commandment greater than these."

Matthew 7:12, NIV

> "In everything, do to others what you would have them do to you, for this sums up the Law and the Prophets."

Luke 7:40–47, NIV

> "Two men owed money to a certain moneylender . . . Neither of them had the money to pay him back, so he canceled the debts of both. Now which of them will love him more?" Simon replied, "I suppose the one who had the bigger debt canceled." "You have judged correctly," Jesus said. . . . "Therefore, I tell you, **her many sins have been forgiven—for she loved much.** But he who has been forgiven little loves little."

Proverbs 3:27, NKJV

> Do not withhold good from those to whom it is due, when it is in the power of your hand to do so.

1 John 3:18, NIV

> Let us not love with words or tongue but with actions and in truth.

Galatians 6:9, NIV

> Let us not become weary in doing good, for at the proper time we will reap a harvest if we do not give up.

85. Marriage Cloaked in Love

(Spouse's Name) and I are one in the eyes of God, and we share in His promises together. We strive to live together harmoniously. Our marital relationship is cloaked in love. We are patient and kind to one another. We are polite and treat each other with respect. We are not envious, jealous, or condescending toward the other. We are not easily angered, and we are quick to forgive, keeping no record of wrongs. We rejoice in the truth, always trusting and protecting each other. We are not self-seeking, but rather have an "attitude of servitude" toward each other. **Our love never fails.**

We have made a covenant with our eyes not to lust after any other. We honor each other and keep our marriage bed pure, not fantasizing about others. We belong to each other, and our desire is intensified for each other. We uphold our banner of love over our marriage, displayed for all to see.

Genesis 2:24, NKJV

A man . . . and . . . his wife . . . shall become one flesh.

Romans 14:19, NASB

Pursue the things which make for peace and the building up of one another.

Colossians 3:14, NKJV

Above all these things put on love, which is the bond of perfection.

1 Corinthians 13:4–8, NIV

Love is patient, love is kind. It does not envy, it does not boast, it is not proud. It is not rude, it is not self-seeking, it is not easily angered, it keeps no record of wrongs. Love does not delight in evil but rejoices with the truth. It always protects, always trusts, always hopes, always perseveres. Love never fails.

Job 31:1–12, AMP

I dictated a covenant (an agreement) to my eyes: how then could I look [lustfully] upon a girl? For what portion should I have from God above [if I were lewd], and what heritage from the Almighty on high? . . . Does not [God] see my ways and count all my steps? . . . For [uncontrolled passion] is a fire . . . [that fire once lighted would rage until all is consumed] and would burn to the root all my [life's] increase.

Hebrews 13:4, NIV

Marriage should be honored by all, and the marriage bed kept pure, for God will judge the adulterer and all the sexually immoral.

86. Mercy Never Fails

Loving Father God, I praise You with all of my soul. I will not forget all of Your benefits. You forgive all my iniquities and heal my diseases. You redeem my life from destruction and crown me with Your love and tender mercies. You are the God of new beginnings. Your mercy never fails; Your compassions are new every morning. Praise Your holy name!

You have not dealt with me according to my sins. As far as the heavens are above the earth, so great is Your mercy toward me! As far as the east is from the west, so far have You removed my transgressions from me. As the most loving earthly father would pity his children, so You have pitied me. You know my frame; You remember I am but dust.

When I confess my sins, You are faithful and just to forgive me my sins and cleanse me of all unrighteousness. Because You delight in mercy, You do not remain angry with me; rather you subdue my iniquities, bringing them under Your control. You cast all of my sins into the depths of the sea. Hallelujah! Thank You, Father!

Psalm 103:1–4, NKJV

Bless the LORD, O my soul; and all that is within me, bless His holy name! Bless the LORD, O my soul, and forget not all His benefits: who forgives all your iniquities, who heals all your diseases, who redeems your life from destruction, who crowns you with lovingkindness and tender mercies.

Lamentations 3:22, 23, NKJV

Through the LORD's mercies we are not consumed, because His compassions fail not. They are new every morning; great is Your faithfulness.

Psalm 103:10–14, NKJV

He has not dealt with us according to our sins, nor punished us according to our iniquities. For as the heavens are high above the earth, so great is His mercy toward those who fear Him; as far as the east is from the west, so far has He removed our transgressions from us. As a father pities his children, so the LORD pities those who fear Him. For He knows our frame; He remembers that we are dust.

Micah 7:18, 19, NKJV

Who is a God like You, pardoning iniquity and passing over the transgression of the remnant of His heritage? He does not retain His anger forever, because He delights in mercy. He will again have compassion on us, and will subdue our iniquities. You will cast all our sins into the depths of the sea

87. The Mind of Christ—Renewed, Re-created

My mind is renewed—my attitudes are made new (and radically changed) through the power of His Word. His Word sanctifies me, separating me from the world's viewpoint. I am set apart morally, ethically, and attitudinally from the world system. My conduct and my thoughts are governed by God's administrative system of His holy kingdom, as recorded in His Word.

I am re-created in the image of God. I have been given the mind of Christ. By the power of the Holy Spirit, I take every thought captive and make it obedient to the will of Christ, my Lord.

Romans 12:2, NKJV

Do not be conformed to this world, but be transformed by the renewing of your mind, that you may prove what is that good and acceptable and perfect will of God.

John 17:17, NKJV

"Sanctify them by Your truth. Your word is truth."

Ephesians 4:22–24, AMP

Strip yourselves of your former nature [put off and discard your old unrenewed self] which characterized your previous manner of life and becomes corrupt through lusts and desires that spring from delusion. And be constantly renewed in the spirit of your mind [having a fresh mental and spiritual attitude], **and put on the new nature (the regenerate self) created in God's image,** [Godlike] in true righteousness and holiness.

Ephesians 2:10, AMP

For we are God's [own] handiwork (His workmanship), recreated in Christ Jesus, [born anew] that we may do those good works which God predestined (planned beforehand) for us.

1 Corinthians 2:16, NKJV

We have the mind of Christ.

2 Corinthians 10:4, 5, NKJV

The weapons of our warfare are not carnal but mighty in God for pulling down strongholds, casting down arguments and every high thing that exalts itself against the knowledge of God, bringing every thought into captivity to the obedience of Christ.

88. Muzzle Your Mouth

I muzzle my mouth, restraining my mouth from sin, as with a bridle over my tongue. By my words I am acquitted; by my words I am condemned:

- I speak in faith, not in doubt and disbelief. Without faith it is impossible to please God.
- I do not lie.
- I do not grumble, murmur, and complain about my circumstances.
- I do everything without arguing or complaining.
- I do not speak with bitterness, rage, or anger—nor do I let any unwholesome talk come from my mouth. In my anger, I do not sin.
- I do not exalt myself by bragging.
- I do not criticize, gossip, repeat rumors, betray another's trust, or enter into godless chatter. "A closed mouth gathers no foot!"
- I do not participate in coarse joking, cursing, or obscenities.
- I do not manipulate others by insincere speech.

Psalm 39:1, AMP

I said, I will take heed and guard my ways, that I may **sin not** with my tongue; I will muzzle my mouth as with a bridle.

Matthew 12:36, 37, AMP

I tell you, on the day of judgment men will have to give account for every idle (inoperative, nonworking) word they speak. For by your words you will be justified and acquitted, and by your words you will be condemned and sentenced.

Romans 14:23, NKJV

Whatever is not from faith is sin.

Hebrews 11:6, NKJV

Without faith it is impossible to please Him, for he who comes to God must believe that He is, and that He is a rewarder of those who diligently seek Him.

John 8:44, NKJV

"You are of your father the devil, and the desires of your father you want to do. He was a murderer from the beginning, and does not stand in the truth, because there is no truth in him. When he speaks a lie, he speaks from his own resources, for he is a liar and the father of it."

1 Corinthians 10:10, NIV

Do not grumble.

Exodus 16:8, AMP

Moses said . . . because the Lord has heard your grumblings which you murmur against Him; what are we? Your murmurings are not against us, but against the LORD.

Philippians 2:14, 15, NKJV

Do all things without complaining and disputing, that you may become blameless and harmless, children of God without fault.

Ephesians 4:29, NKJV

Let no corrupt word proceed out of your mouth, but what is good for necessary edification, that it may impart grace to the hearers.

Ephesians 4:25–27, NIV

Each of you must put off falsehood and speak truthfully to his neighbor, for we are all members of one body. "In your anger do not sin": Do not let the sun go down while you are still angry, and do not give the devil a foothold.

Psalm 94:4, NIV

They pour out arrogant words; all the evildoers are full of boasting.

Leviticus 19:16, AMP

You shall not go up and down as a dispenser of gossip and scandal among your people.

Proverbs 11:13, AMP

He who goes about as a talebearer reveals secrets, but he who is trustworthy and faithful in spirit keeps the matter hidden.

2 Timothy 2:16, NKJV

Shun profane and idle babblings, for they will increase to more ungodliness.

Ephesians 5:4, AMP

Let there be no filthiness (obscenity, indecency) nor foolish and sinful (silly and corrupt) talk, nor coarse jesting, which are not fitting or becoming.

Jude 16, NKJV

These are grumblers, complainers, walking according to their own lusts; and they mouth great swelling words, flattering people to gain advantage.

89. A New Creation in Christ

I am a new creation in Christ Jesus. I do not dwell on the past, for God is doing a new thing in me. I release my past and press forward. My old nature has vanished; now only my new Christlike nature exists.

Although I have yet to attain my destiny to become like Christ, I am keeping my eyes on the goal and pressing forward—forgetting what is behind and reaching out for what is ahead. God gives me life and foresees the result of His life at work within me. I am counting on Him to complete my transformation, considering it a "done deal" in Christ.

2 Corinthians 5:17, NKJV

If anyone is in Christ, he is a new creation; old things have passed away; behold, all things have become new.

Isaiah 43:18, 19, NIV

"Forget the former things; do not dwell on the past. See, I am doing a new thing! Now it springs up; do you not perceive it?"

Philippians 3:13, 14, NIV

I do not consider myself yet to have taken hold of it. But one thing I do: Forgetting what is behind and straining toward what is ahead, I press on toward the goal to win the prize for which God has called me heavenward in Christ Jesus.

Romans 4:17, NKJV

God, who gives life to the dead and calls those things which do not exist as though they did.

Philippians 1:6, AMP

I am convinced and sure of this very thing, that He Who began a good work in you will continue until the day of Jesus Christ [right up to the time of His return], developing [that good work] and perfecting and bringing it to full completion in you.

90. Obedience—My Covenant Response

God has written His laws in my heart. Because I love Him, I am walking in covenant obedience. Christ Jesus is my covenant with God. I keep covenant by abiding in Christ and His Word—keeping His commandments, by the power of His Holy Spirit. I practice righteousness. I will not be ashamed at His coming! I continue in the goodness of God, and I will not be cut off.

God does not change—He keeps covenant with those who keep covenant with Him. I have eternal life because I have Jesus. My covenant response to His love is to obey God and remain faithful to Jesus. God counts me among His saints.

Hebrews 10:16, NKJV

"This is the covenant that I will make with them after those days, says the LORD: I will put My laws into their hearts, and in their minds I will write them."

John 14:23, 24, NIV

Jesus replied, "If anyone loves me, he will obey my teaching. . . . He who does not love me will not obey my teaching."

Isaiah 42:6, 7, AMP

I the Lord have called You [the Messiah] for a righteous purpose and in righteousness; I will take You by the hand and will keep You; I will give You for a covenant to the people [Israel], for a light to the nations [Gentiles], to open the eyes of the blind, to bring out prisoners from the dungeon, and those who sit in darkness from the prison.

John 8:31, 32, NKJV

Jesus said to those Jews who believed Him, "If you abide in My word, you are My disciples indeed. And you shall know the truth, and the truth shall make you free."

Hebrews 5:9, NKJV

"Having been perfected, He became the author of eternal salvation to all who obey Him."

1 John 3:24, NASB

The one who keeps His commandments abides in Him, and He in him. We know by this that He abides in us, by the Spirit whom He has given us.

Acts 5:32, NKJV

"We are His witnesses to these things, and so also is the Holy Spirit whom God has given to those who obey Him."

1 John 2:28, 29, NKJV

Now, little children, abide in Him, that when He appears, we may have confidence and not be ashamed before Him at His coming. If you know that He is righteous, you know that everyone who practices righteousness is born of Him.

Romans 11:20–22, NKJV

Because of unbelief they were broken off, and you stand by faith. Do not be haughty, but fear. For if God did not spare the natural branches, He may not spare you either. Therefore consider the goodness and severity of God: on those who fell, severity; but toward you, goodness, if you continue in His goodness. Otherwise you also will be cut off.

Malachi 3:6, AMP

I am the Lord, I do not change.

Nehemiah 9:7, 8, NKJV

"You are the LORD . . . who chose Abram . . . and gave him the name Abraham; You found his heart faithful before You, and made a covenant with him. . . . You have performed Your words, for You are righteous."

Genesis 26:4, 5, NKJV

"In your seed all the nations . . . shall be blessed; because Abraham obeyed My voice and kept . . . My commandments . . . and My laws."

Exodus 19:5, 6, NKJV

" 'If you will indeed obey My voice and keep My covenant, then you shall be a special treasure to Me . . . a kingdom of priests and a holy nation.' "

Deuteronomy 7:9, NKJV

"Know that the LORD your God, He is God, the faithful God who keeps covenant and mercy . . . with those who love Him and keep His commandments."

John 3:36, AMP

And he who believes in (has faith in, clings to, relies on) the Son has (now possesses) eternal life. But whoever disobeys (is unbelieving toward, refuses to trust in, disregards, is not subject to) the Son will never see (experience) life, but [instead] the wrath of God abides on him.

Revelation 14:12, NIV

This calls for patient endurance on the part of the saints who obey God's commandments and remain faithful to Jesus.

91. Obedience Demonstrates My Love for God

This is how I demonstrate my love for God:
- **I obey His commandments.**
- **I put His Word into practice.**

I am held accountable for that which He has revealed to me. If I said "I know Him" but refused to keep His commandments, God would regard me as a liar. I conduct my life according to the truth He has revealed to me from the Bible.

John 14:15, NKJV

"If you love Me, keep My commandments."

1 John 5:3, 4, NIV

This is love for God: **to obey his commands.** And his commands are not burdensome, for everyone born of God overcomes the world. This is the victory that has overcome the world, even our faith.

Luke 8:21, NIV

He replied, "My mother and brothers are those who **hear** God's word and **put it into practice.**"

1 Corinthians 4:2, NIV

It is required that those who have been given a trust must prove faithful.

Romans 14:23, AMP

Whatever does not originate and proceed from faith is sin [whatever is done without a conviction of its **approval by God** is sinful].

1 John 2:3, 4, NKJV

By this we know that we know Him, if we keep His commandments. He who says, "I know Him," and does not keep His commandments, is a liar, and the truth is not in him.

Philippians 3:16, AMP

Let us hold true to what we have already attained and walk and order our lives by that.

92. Obedience Is the Pathway to Blessing

Obedience is the pathway to God's blessing. I am blessed because I am a doer of the Word. I put His Word into practice. God teaches me to profit and leads me in the way I should go. His peace flows through me like a river, and His righteousness like waves of the sea.

All of His promises are mine in Christ Jesus, but they are conditional. I must persevere, so that **after I have done His will** I may receive the promise. Because I keep His commandments, I have confidence before God and receive from Him what I ask.

Luke 11:28, AMP

He said, **Blessed . . .** are those who hear the Word of God and **obey and practice** it!

James 1:25, NIV

The man who looks intently into the perfect law that gives freedom, and continues to do this, not forgetting what he has heard, but doing it—he will be blessed in what he does.

Psalm 119:1–3, NASB

How blessed are those whose way is blameless, who walk in the law of the LORD. How blessed are those who observe His testimonies, who seek Him with all their heart. They also do no unrighteousness; they walk in His ways.

Isaiah 48:17, 18, NKJV

"I am the LORD your God, who teaches you to profit, who leads you by the way you should go. Oh, that you had heeded My commandments! Then your peace would have been like a river, and your righteousness like the waves of the sea."

2 Corinthians 1:20, AMP

For as many as are the promises of God, they all find their Yes [answer] in Him [Christ]. For this reason we also utter the Amen (so be it) to God through Him.

Hebrews 10:36, NKJV

For you have need of endurance, so that after you have done the will of God, you may receive the promise.

1 John 3:21, 22, NASB

Beloved, if our heart does not condemn us, we have confidence before God; and whatever we ask we receive from Him, because we keep His commandments and do the things that are pleasing in His sight.

93. Overcome the World

I find joy in fulfilling God's commandments and His counsel; my obedience is born from my love for Him. My faith is the victory that conquers and overcomes the satanic principles that rule the world system. Walking in faith of the power of Christ in me, I have continuous victory over all struggles with sin.

Jesus came to earth to destroy the devil's works. In partaking of my humanity and dying my death on Calvary's cross, He conquered Satan's power, making a public spectacle of him and his unholy alliance. Christ overcame the world system. He now gives me power over the enemy.

By the blood of the Lamb and the word of my testimony, I overcome the devil. I am more than a conqueror through Christ who loves me!

1 John 5:3, 4, NKJV

This is the love of God, that we keep His commandments. And His commandments are not burdensome. For whatever is born of God overcomes the world. And this is the victory that has overcome the world—our faith.

1 John 3:8, NASB

The Son of God appeared for this purpose, to destroy the works of the devil.

Hebrews 2:14, 15, NASB

Since the children share in flesh and blood, He Himself likewise also partook of the same, that through death He might render powerless him who had the power of death, that is, the devil, and might free those who through fear of death were subject to slavery all their lives.

Colossians 2:15, NKJV

Having disarmed principalities and powers, He made a public spectacle of them, triumphing over them in it.

Revelation 12:11, NKJV

"They overcame him by the blood of the Lamb and by the word of their testimony."

Romans 8:37, AMP

Yet amid all these things we are more than conquerors and gain a surpassing victory through Him Who loved us.

94. The Overcomer's Reward Is Mine

By the grace of God, I will overcome to the end! I will be clothed in white garments—His robe of righteousness—and Jesus will not blot my name from the Book of Life.

Jesus Christ, my Savior, will give me the overcomer's reward. I will eat from the tree of life and receive hidden manna. He will write my new name on a white stone, proving my acquittal from guilt. I will be a pillar in the temple of God—having a permanent place in His presence—and Christ will inscribe God's name and His new name on me.

I am overcoming Satan by the blood of the Lamb and the word of my testimony. I shall inherit all things, and God will be my heavenly Father throughout eternity.

Revelation 3:5, NKJV

"He who overcomes shall be clothed in white garments, and I will not blot out his name from the Book of Life; but I will confess his name before My Father and before His angels."

Revelation 2:7, NKJV

"To him who overcomes I will give to eat from the tree of life, which is in the midst of the Paradise of God."

Revelation 2:17, NKJV

"To him who overcomes I will give some of the hidden manna to eat. And I will give him a white stone, and on the stone a new name written which no one knows except him who receives it."

Revelation 2:26, NKJV

"He who overcomes, and keeps My works until the end, to him I will give power over the nations."

Revelation 3:12, NKJV

"He who overcomes, I will make him a pillar in the temple of My God . . . I will write on him the name of My God and . . . I will write on him My new name."

Revelation 12:11, NKJV

"And they overcame him by the blood of the Lamb and by the word of their testimony."

Revelation 21:7, NKJV

"He who overcomes shall inherit all things, and I will be his God and he shall be My son."

95. Partaker of the Divine Nature

I am partaking of God's divine nature by holding fast to His promises.
I am planting God's promises in my heart to ensure I don't sin against Him.
All of God's promises are mine, "yes" and "amen" ("so be it"), **in Christ.** I eagerly anticipate the fulfillment of God's promises. This hope is an anchor for my soul, keeping me from being double minded.
Through obedience (doing His will), faith, and patience, I am confident I will receive what my Father has promised.

2 Peter 1:3, 4, NIV

His divine power has given us everything we need for life and godliness through our knowledge of him who called us by his own glory and goodness. . . . He has given us **his very great and precious promises,** so that **through them you may participate in the divine nature** and escape the corruption in the world caused by evil desires.

Psalm 119:11, NKJV

Your word I have hidden in my heart, that I might not sin against You!

2 Corinthians 1:20, NIV

No matter how many promises God has made, they are "Yes" in Christ.

Hebrews 6:17–19, NIV

Because God wanted to make the unchanging nature of his purpose very clear to the heirs of what was promised, he confirmed it with an oath. God did this so that, by two unchangeable things in which it is impossible for God to lie, we who have fled to take hold of the hope offered to us may be greatly encouraged. **We have this hope as an anchor for the soul, firm and secure.**

Hebrews 10:36–38, NKJV

For you have need of endurance, so that **after you have done the will of God, you may receive the promise:** "For yet a little while, and He who is coming will come and will not tarry. Now the just shall live by faith; but if anyone draws back, My soul has no pleasure in him."

Hebrews 6:12, NKJV

Do not become sluggish, but imitate those who through faith and patience inherit the promises.

96. Perfect Peace

I am walking in constant peace—His peace that guards my heart in all circumstances and is beyond human understanding. **God keeps me in perfect peace,** because my mind has a steadfast trust in His faithfulness.

God is not the author of confusion. Whenever I begin to feel stressed and anxious, I realize my eyes are not focused on my Lord. I return my thoughts to Him and place my complete trust in Him. He restores my peace, causing me to overflow with hope by the power of His Spirit.

Philippians 4:6, 7, NKJV

Be anxious for nothing, but in everything by prayer and supplication, with thanksgiving, let your requests be made known to God; and **the peace of God,** which surpasses all understanding, will guard your hearts and minds through Christ Jesus.

Isaiah 26:3, NKJV

"You will keep him in perfect peace, whose mind is stayed on You, because he trusts in You."

John 14:27, AMP

Peace I leave with you; My [own] peace I now give and bequeath to you. Not as the world gives do I give to you. Do not let your hearts be troubled, neither let them be afraid.

1 Corinthians 14:33, KJV

God is not the author of confusion, but of peace.

Isaiah 30:15, AMP

Thus said the Lord God, the Holy One of Israel: In returning [to Me] and resting [in Me] you shall be saved; in quietness and in [trusting] confidence shall be your strength.

Isaiah 32:17, NIV

The fruit of righteousness will be **peace;** the effect of righteousness will be quietness and confidence forever.

Romans 15:13, NIV

May the God of hope fill you with all **joy and peace** as you trust in him, so that you may overflow with hope by the power of the Holy Spirit.

97. Plans Committed to God Succeed

Whatever I do, I commit my plans to the Lord, and He causes them to succeed. Apart from Him, I can do nothing.
My hard work brings a profit. My success increases because I have many godly advisors. I seek the Lord, and He directs my steps, leading me in the way I should go. I commit my days into God's hands; He gives me strength and power for a victorious life.

Proverbs 16:3, NIV

Commit to the LORD whatever you do, and your plans will succeed.

Psalm 37:5, NKJV

Commit your way to the LORD, trust also in Him, and He shall bring it to pass.

John 15:5, NASB

"Apart from Me you can do nothing."

Proverbs 14:23, NIV

All hard work brings a profit, but mere talk leads only to poverty.

Proverbs 15:22, NIV

Plans fail for lack of counsel, but with many advisers they succeed.

Psalm 37:23, AMP

The steps of a [good] man are directed and established by the Lord when He delights in his way [and He busies Himself with his every step].

Isaiah 48:17, 18, NKJV

"I am the LORD your God, who teaches you to profit, who leads you by the way you should go. Oh, that you had heeded My commandments! Then your peace would have been like a river, and your righteousness like the waves of the sea."

1 Chronicles 29:11–13, AMP

Yours, O Lord, is the greatness and the power and the glory and the victory and the majesty, for all that is in the heavens and the earth is Yours; Yours is the kingdom, O Lord, and Yours it is to be exalted as Head over all. **Both riches and honor come from You, and You reign over all. In Your hands are power and might; in Your hands it is to make great and to give strength to all. Now therefore, our God, we thank You and praise Your glorious name** and those attributes which that name denotes.

98. Plugged in to Your Power Source

By the power of His Word and His Holy Spirit, my Father lights up every area of my life and eliminates the darkness of my soul. He lights the lamp of my inner being and causes me to shine with His radiance. God is my strength and power and makes my way perfect. **I stay "plugged in" to my power source and He gives my life true purpose.**

Psalm 119:130, NKJV

The entrance of Your words gives light; it gives understanding to the simple.

Psalm 18:28, NKJV

For You will light my lamp; the LORD my God will enlighten my darkness.

Ephesians 5:14, AMP

Therefore He says, Awake, O sleeper, and arise from the dead, and Christ shall shine (make day dawn) upon you and give you light.

Isaiah 60:1, AMP

ARISE [from the depression and prostration in which circumstances have kept you—rise to a new life]! Shine (be radiant with the glory of the Lord), for your light has come, and the glory of the Lord has risen upon you!

2 Samuel 22:33, NKJV

God is my strength and power, and He makes my way perfect.

99. Positioned "in Christ Jesus"

I am positioned "in Christ Jesus." Because I have received Christ as my Savior, I now have a spiritual union with Him. The "law of the Spirit of life" works in me.

When I look into the Word of God, I begin to see a vision—a reflection—of who I am in Christ. When I think and act according to the Word, I am blessed in whatever I do.

Ephesians 1:13, 14, NIV

> **You also were included in Christ** when you heard the word of truth, the gospel of your salvation. Having believed, you were marked in him with a seal, the promised Holy Spirit, who is a deposit guaranteeing our inheritance until the redemption of those who are God's possession.

1 Corinthians 1:30, AMP

> It is from Him that you have your life **in Christ Jesus**, Whom God has made **our Wisdom** from God, . . . **our Righteousness** [. . . putting us in right standing with God], and **our Consecration** [making us pure and holy], and **our Redemption** [providing our ransom from the eternal penalty for sin].

1 Corinthians 6:17, NKJV

> He who is joined to the Lord is one spirit with Him.

Romans 7:23–8:2, AMP

> I discern in my bodily members [in the sensitive appetites and wills of the flesh] a **different law** (rule of action) at war against the law of my mind . . . and making me a prisoner to the **law of sin. . . .** Who will release and deliver me from [the shackles of] this body of death? O thank God! [He will!] through Jesus Christ . . . our Lord! . . . For the **law of the Spirit of life** [which is] in Christ Jesus [the law of our new being] has freed me from the **law of sin** and of death.

James 1:23–25, NIV

> **Anyone who listens to the word** but does not do what it says is like a man who **looks at his face in a mirror** and, after looking at himself, goes away and immediately forgets what he looks like. But the man who looks intently into the perfect law that gives freedom, and continues to do this, not forgetting what he has heard, but doing it—he will be blessed in what he does.

100. Potential of the Harvest

I am born again by the life-giving and everlasting Word of God and the power of His Spirit. Almighty God is my "Abba" Father. His Word is incorruptible seed.

The potential of any harvest is in the seed. All my potential is wrapped inside His Seed—His Holy Word, which is powerfully at work within me.

John 3:5–7, NIV

"I tell you the truth, no one can enter the kingdom of God unless he is born of water and the Spirit. Flesh gives birth to flesh, but the Spirit gives birth to spirit. You should not be surprised at my saying, 'You must be born again.' "

1 Peter 1:22, 23, NKJV

Since you have purified your souls in obeying the truth through the Spirit . . . having been born again, not of corruptible seed but incorruptible, through the Word of God which lives and abides forever.

Luke 8:11, NIV

"This is the meaning of the parable: The seed is the word of God."

James 1:18–21, AMP

It was of His own [free] will that **He gave us birth . . . by [His] Word of Truth. . . .** So get rid of all uncleanness and the rampant outgrowth of wickedness, and in a humble (gentle, modest) spirit receive and welcome the Word which implanted and rooted [in your hearts] contains the power to save your souls.

1 Thessalonians 2:13, AMP

And we also [especially] thank God continually for this, that when you received the message of God [which you heard] from us, you welcomed it not as the word of [mere] men, but as it truly is, **the Word of God, which is effectually at work in you who believe** [exercising its superhuman power in those who adhere to and trust in and rely on it].

101. The Power of the Spirit Within Me

God enlightens my understanding to know the hope to which He has called me and the inheritance He has laid up for me. His power that worked so mightily to raise my crucified Savior, is now working in my heart. He has given me a spirit of power, exchanging His strength for my weakness and making His power perfect in me.

I can do everything through Christ who strengthens me with power through His Holy Spirit. He is able to do abundantly more than I can imagine, according to His power working within me. I live my life not by human strength, but by the power of His Spirit.

Ephesians 1:18–20, NKJV

That you may know what is the hope of His calling, what are the riches of the glory of His inheritance in the saints, and what is the exceeding greatness of His power toward us who believe, according to the working of His mighty power which He worked in Christ when He raised Him from the dead and seated Him at His right hand in the heavenly places.

2 Timothy 1:7, NKJV

God has not given us a spirit of fear, but of power and of love and of a sound mind.

Isaiah 40:29, 31, NKJV

He gives power to the weak, and to those who have no might He increases strength. . . . Those who wait on the Lord shall renew their strength; they shall mount up with wings like eagles, they shall run and not be weary.

2 Corinthians 12:9, NIV

"My grace is sufficient for you, for my power is made perfect in weakness."

Philippians 4:13, NKJV

I can do all things through Christ who strengthens me.

Ephesians 3:16–21, NASB

That He would grant you . . . to be strengthened with power through His Spirit in the inner man. . . . Now to Him who is able to do far more abundantly beyond all that we ask or think, according to the power that works within us, to Him be the glory in the church and in Christ Jesus.

Zechariah 4:6, NIV

" 'Not by might nor by power, but by my Spirit,' " says the Lord Almighty.

102. Power for Transformation

God's way is perfect, and His word, proven. By His divine power, I have been given everything I need for abundant life and godliness. He has given me exceedingly great and precious promises. Through these promises, I am a partaker of His divine nature. It is also through these promises that I escape the clutches of corruption.

His word is living and powerful. He gave me life through His word, which is exercising its transforming power in me now. By His Word, I am revived. He sends forth His word to heal me and rescue me from the pit of destruction. God sanctifies me by His Holy Scriptures. I lay up His word in my heart that I might not sin against Him. It is by His word that I avoid the paths of the destroyer.

Before I was afflicted; I went astray. But now I receive and obey His word. It is a guide for my footsteps and enlightens the pathway of my future. The entrance of His word brings light and directs me in the way that is pleasing to Him.

His word dwells in me richly. I am not conformed to the world. The power of His word renews my mind to understand God's perfect will. I rise early each morning to meditate on His word, which is a treasure of transforming power.

2 Samuel 22:31, NKJV

As for God, His way is perfect; the word of the LORD is proven.

2 Peter 1:3, 4, NKJV

His divine power has given to us all things that pertain to life and godliness, through the knowledge of Him who called us by glory and virtue, by which have been given to us exceedingly great and precious promises, that through these you may be partakers of the divine nature, having escaped the corruption that is in the world through lust.

Hebrews 4:12, NKJV

The word of God is living and powerful.

Psalm 119:50, NKJV

Your word has given me life.

1 Peter 1:23, NKJV

Having been born again, not of corruptible seed but incorruptible, through the word of God which lives and abides forever.

1 Thessalonians 2:13, AMP

You welcomed it not as the word of [mere] men, but as it truly is, the Word of God, which is effectually at work in you who believe [exercising its superhuman power in those who adhere to and trust in and rely on it].

Psalm 119:154, NKJV

Plead my cause and redeem me; revive me according to Your word.

Psalm 107:20, AMP

He sends forth His word and heals them and rescues them from the pit and destruction.

John 17:17, NKJV

"Sanctify them by the truth. Your word is truth."

Psalm 119:11, AMP

Your word have I laid up in my heart, that I might not sin against You.

Psalm 17:4, NKJV

By the word of Your lips, I have kept away from the paths of the destroyer.

Psalm 119:67, AMP

Before I was afflicted I went astray, but now Your word do I keep [hearing, receiving, loving, and obeying it].

Psalm 119:105, NKJV

Your word is a lamp to my feet and a light to my path.

Psalm 119:130–133, AMP

The entrance and unfolding of Your words give light; their unfolding gives understanding (discernment and comprehension) to the simple. . . . Establish my steps and direct them by [means of] Your word; let not any iniquity have dominion over me.

Romans 12:2, NASB

Do not be conformed to this world, but be transformed by the renewing of your mind, so that you may prove what the will of God is, that which is good and acceptable and perfect.

Psalm 119:148, AMP

My eyes anticipate the night watches and I am awake before the cry of the watchman, that I may meditate on Your word.

103. Pray Boldly Before His Throne of Grace

I come boldly before God's throne of grace to obtain mercy and help in time of need. Because I obey His commands, do what pleases Him, ask with unselfish motives and in agreement with His will, His ears are attentive to my prayers.

I have this confidence in approaching my holy and righteous Father. He hears my prayers. By His love, power, and faithfulness, I have what I ask of Him in the authority of Jesus' name.

Hebrews 4:15, 16, NKJV

We do not have a High Priest who cannot sympathize with our weaknesses, but was in all points tempted as we are, yet without sin. Let us therefore come boldly to the throne of grace, that we may obtain mercy and find grace to help in time of need.

1 John 3:21, 22, NIV

Dear friends, if our hearts do not condemn us, we have confidence before God and receive from him anything we ask, because we obey his commands and do what pleases him.

James 4:2, 3, AMP

You do not have, because you do not ask God. [Or] you do ask [God for them] and yet fail to receive, because you ask with wrong purpose and evil, selfish motives.

1 John 5:14, NKJV

This is the confidence that we have in Him, that if we ask anything according to His will, He hears us.

1 Peter 3:12, AMP

The eyes of the Lord are upon the righteous (those who are upright and in right standing with God), and His ears are attentive to their prayer. But the face of the Lord is against those who practice evil [to oppose them, to frustrate, and defeat them].

2 Chronicles 16:9, NKJV

For the eyes of the LORD run to and fro throughout the whole earth, to show Himself strong on behalf of those whose heart is loyal to Him.

John 16:23, 24, NKJV

"Whatever you ask the Father in My name He will give you. Until now you have asked nothing in My name. Ask, and you will receive, that your joy may be full."

104. Pressing on for the Prize

The Lord has begun a great work in me, and He will be faithful to complete it. His gifts and His calling on my life are offered without any regret on His part. He does not change His mind about what He makes available to me.

I work out the salvation God has placed in me—not in my own strength, but by co-operating in His purposes for my life. By the transforming power of His Word and His Spirit, God is working in me to cause me to be all that He has called me to be.

I may not be perfect yet, but I am forgetting my past and straining toward my future. I press on toward the goal to win the prize for which God has called me heavenward in Christ Jesus.

Philippians 1:6, AMP

And I am convinced and sure of this very thing, **that He who began a good work in you will continue until the day of Christ Jesus** [right up to the time of His return], developing [that good work] and perfecting and bringing it to full completion in you.

Romans 11:29, NKJV

The gifts and the calling of God are irrevocable.

Philippians 2:12, 13, AMP

Work out (cultivate, carry out to the goal, and fully complete) your own salvation with reverence and awe and trembling (self-distrust, with serious caution, tenderness of conscience, watchfulness against temptation, timidly shrinking from whatever might offend God and discredit the name of Christ). [Not in your own strength] for it is God Who is all the while effectually at work in you [energizing and creating in you the power and desire], both to will and to work for His good pleasure and satisfaction and delight.

Philippians 3:12–14, NIV

Not that I have already obtained all this, or have already been made perfect, but I press on to take hold of that for which Christ Jesus took hold of me. Brothers, I do not consider myself yet to have taken hold of it. But one thing I do: Forgetting what is behind and straining toward what is ahead, I press on toward the goal to win the prize for which God has called me heavenward in Christ Jesus.

105. Redeem My Time

Father, I am Your "work of art," recreated in Christ to do the good works You prepared in advance for me to do. I pray You will teach me to number my days correctly and to realize how short my time is here on earth. Cause me to be sensitive to the still small voice of Your Holy Spirit and to respond rapidly. Please forgive me for the sin of procrastination, Lord.

Lord, by Your power I will make the most of every opportunity. My conversation will be gracious and seasoned with salt. I will witness to others, explaining the hope I find in You.

Teach me to redeem my time and use it for Your good purposes.

Ephesians 2:10, NIV

We are God's workmanship, created in Christ Jesus to do good works, which God prepared in advance for us to do.

Psalm 90:12, AMP

Teach us to number our days, that we may get us a heart of wisdom.

Psalm 39:4, AMP

Lord, make me to know my end and [to appreciate] the measure of my days—what it is; let me know and realize how frail I am [how transient is my stay here].

1 Kings 19:12–19, AMP

[A sound of gentle stillness and] a still, small voice. . . . And behold, there came a voice to him and said, What are you doing here, Elijah? . . . So Elijah left there.

Psalm 95:7, 8, NKJV

Today, if you will hear His voice: "Do not harden your hearts, as in the rebellion, as in the day of trial in the wilderness."

Colossians 4:5, 6, NKJV

Walk in wisdom toward those who are outside, redeeming the time. Let your speech always be with grace, seasoned with salt, that you may know how you ought to answer each one.

Ephesians 5:15, 16, NKJV

See then that you walk circumspectly, not as fools but as wise, redeeming the time, because the days are evil.

106. Redeemed and Saved by God's Grace

I am the redeemed of the Lord, saved by His marvelous grace. Nothing I could do could earn or merit His superabundant favor; it is purely a gift of grace from the Lord.

Thank You, Lord Jesus, for redeeming me. I know I could never save myself! Thank You, Father, for Your gracious gift of life!

Psalm 107:2, NKJV

Let the redeemed of the LORD say so.

Galatians 3:10–13, AMP

All who depend on the Law [who are seeking to be justified by obedience to the **Law of rituals**] are under a curse and doomed to disappointment and destruction, for it is written in the Scriptures, Cursed . . . be everyone who does not continue to abide (live and remain) by all the precepts and commands written in the **Book of the Law** and to practice them. . . . **Christ purchased our freedom** [redeeming us] from the curse (doom) of the law [and its condemnation] by [Himself] becoming a curse for us, for it is written [in the Scriptures]: Cursed is everyone who hangs on a tree (is crucified).

John 3:16, 17, NKJV

"God so loved the world that He gave His only begotten Son, that whoever believes in Him should not perish but have everlasting life. For God did not send His Son into the world to condemn the world, but that the world through Him might be saved."

Roman 5:8, NKJV

God demonstrates His own love toward us, in that while we were still sinners, Christ died for us.

Ephesians 2:4, 5, NIV

Because of his great love for us, God, who is rich in mercy, made us alive with Christ even when we were dead in transgressions—it is by grace you have been saved.

Ephesians 2:8–10, NKJV

By grace you have been saved through faith, and that not of yourselves; it is the gift of God, not of works, lest anyone should boast. For we are His workmanship, created in Christ Jesus for good works, which God prepared beforehand that we should walk in them.

107. Rejoice in His Loving-kindness

Father, I rejoice in Your loving-kindness. I rejoice in Your salvation. Thank You for writing my name in the book of life. I call upon You, trusting that You will make everything beautiful in its time. Thank You for putting eternity in my heart.

How could I help but to rejoice and to do good during my short time on earth? I put my trust in Your unfailing love. I sing of Your goodness and shout for joy because You have saved me.

Because I trust in You, I will rejoice in You always. You, the God of my salvation, fill me with peace—even in the midst of turmoil. Thank You for surrounding me with Your loving-kindness and for giving me cause to rejoice!

Psalm 86:4, 5, NASB

Make glad the soul of Your servant, for to You, O Lord, I lift up my soul. For You, Lord, are good, and ready to forgive, and abundant in lovingkindness to all who call upon You.

Psalm 35:9, NKJV

My soul shall be joyful in the LORD; it shall rejoice in His salvation.

Luke 10:20, NKJV

"Rejoice because your names are written in heaven."

Ecclesiastes 3:10–12, NKJV

I have seen the God-given task with which the sons of men are to be occupied. He has made everything beautiful in its time. Also He has put eternity in their hearts, except that no one can find out the work that God does from beginning to end. I know that nothing is better for them than to rejoice, and to do good in their lives.

Psalm 5:11, AMP

Let all those who take refuge and put their trust in You rejoice; let them ever sing and shout for joy, because You make a covering over them and defend them; let those also who love Your name be joyful in You and be in high spirits.

Psalm 13:5, 6, NIV

I trust in your unfailing love; my heart rejoices in your salvation. I will sing to the LORD, for he has been good to me.

108. Rejoice in the Lord Always

Father, because Your love is better than life, my lips will praise You. My soul shall be joyful in You, precious Lord. I am clothed with Your garments of salvation. I am covered with Your robe of righteousness.

I planted in tears, but I will reap a harvest of joy. Thank You, Father, for filling me with comfort. In all my tribulation, I am exceedingly joyful. My soul magnifies You, Lord; my spirit rejoices in my Savior. I will not be grieved and depressed, for the joy of the Lord is my strength. Thoughts of Your salvation remove the heartache that has crushed my spirit and put a smile on my face. I rejoice in You always, Lord!

Psalm 63:3, AMP

Because Your loving-kindness is better than life, my lips shall praise You.

Isaiah 61:10, NKJV

I will greatly rejoice in the Lord, my soul shall be joyful in my God; for He has clothed me with the garments of salvation, He has covered me with the robe of righteousness, as a bridegroom decks himself with ornaments, and as a bride adorns herself with her jewels.

Psalm 126:5, 6, NIV

Those who sow in tears will reap with songs of joy. He who goes out weeping, carrying seed to sow, will return with songs of joy, carrying sheaves with him.

2 Corinthians 7:4, NKJV

I am filled with comfort. I am exceedingly joyful in all our tribulation.

Luke 1:46, 47, AMP

My soul magnifies and extols the Lord, and my spirit rejoices in God my Savior.

Nehemiah 8:10, AMP

Be not grieved and depressed, for the joy of the Lord is your strength and stronghold.

Proverbs 15:13, NIV

A happy heart makes the face cheerful, but heartache crushes the spirit.

Philippians 4:4, NIV

Rejoice in the Lord always. I will say it again: Rejoice!

109. Relying on His Promise

Father, I am relying on the power of Your Word and Your Spirit to work within me—to cause me to will and to act according to Your good purpose. I gladly confess my weaknesses to You, for Your grace is sufficient. Thank You for making Your power perfect in my weakness.

Just as a branch must be connected to the vine for life and vitality, I know my union to Christ is critical for success. Apart from Christ, I can do nothing—nothing to change myself and nothing of eternal consequence. But by the power of the Holy Spirit, I can put to death the misdeeds of my flesh.

I thank You, Father, for the confidence You have given me in Christ. I can do all things through Christ, who continues to strengthen me day by day. The life of Christ in me (as His temple) is my hope of glory.

Philippians 2:13, NIV

It is God who works in you to will and to act according to his good purpose.

2 Corinthians 12:9, NKJV

He said to me, "My grace is sufficient for you, for My strength is made perfect in weakness."

John 15:5, NASB

"I am the vine, you are the branches; he who abides in Me and I in him, he bears much fruit, for apart from Me you can do nothing."

Jeremiah 13:23, NIV

Can the Ethiopian change his skin or the leopard its spots? Neither can you do good who are accustomed to doing evil.

Romans 8:13, NIV

If you live according to the sinful nature, you will die; but if by the Spirit you put to death the misdeeds of the body, you will live.

Philippians 4:13, NKJV

I can do all things through Christ who strengthens me.

Colossians 1:27, NIV

To them God has chosen to make known among the Gentiles the glorious riches of this mystery, which is Christ in you, the hope of glory.

110. Repentance Is a Gift From God

O Lord, my God, how often have I been crushed and crippled in spirit? Yet You have not broken me off and tossed me away. How often has my spiritual zeal been reduced to a flickering flame that sends an offensive haze of smoke upward? Yet You do not snuff me out. When I shut You out of my heart, You stand at the door and knock. I thank You for Your goodness that leads me to repentance.

I want to repent. Give me a change of heart, cause me to change my conduct, turn me back full-faced to You. Turn me away from self-seeking unrighteousness. I don't want to store up wrath for myself in the day of judgment. Cause me to seek glory, honor, and immortality by obeying the truth.

Lord, grant me repentance and forgiveness of sins. Turn me around! Cause me to cooperate with Your Spirit to put to death the misdeeds of my flesh. Thank You, Lord, for the answer to the prayer of faith. Thank You for leading me by Your good Spirit.

Matthew 12:20, NKJV

"A bruised reed He will not break, and smoking flax He will not quench."

Revelation 3:19, 20, NKJV

"As many as I love, I rebuke and chasten. Therefore be zealous and repent. Behold, I stand at the door and knock. If anyone hears My voice and opens the door, I will come in to him and dine with him, and he with Me."

Romans 2:4–7, NKJV

Do you despise the riches of His goodness, forbearance, and long-suffering, not knowing that the goodness of God leads you to repentance? . . . God . . . "will render" . . . eternal life to those who by patient continuance in doing good seek for glory, honor, and immortality.

Acts 5:31, NKJV

"Him God has exalted to His right hand to be Prince and Savior, to give repentance to Israel and forgiveness of sins."

Romans 8:13, NIV

For if you live according to the sinful nature, you will die; but if by the Spirit you put to death the misdeeds of the body, you will live,

Psalm 143:10, NASB

Teach me to do Your will, For You are my God; Let Your good Spirit lead me on level ground.

111. Repentance Results in Refreshing

I confess my sins of commission (that which I did, but should not have done) and my sins of omission (that which I did not do, but should have done) with confidence that God will forgive me and cleanse me from all unrighteousness. By God's power, I turn away from my sins in repentance and turn to Him in faith. He wipes out my sins and gives me glorious times of refreshing.

1 John 1:9, NKJV

If we confess our sins, He is faithful and just to forgive us our sins and to cleanse us from all unrighteousness.

1 John 3:4, AMP

Everyone who commits (practices) sin is guilty of lawlessness; for [that is what] sin is, lawlessness (the breaking, violating of God's law by transgression or neglect—being unrestrained and unregulated by His commands and His will).

1 John 5:17, AMP

All wrongdoing is sin.

Romans 14:23, AMP

Whatever does not originate and proceed from faith is sin [whatever is done without a conviction of its approval by God is sinful].

James 4:17, AMP

Any person who knows what is right to do but does not do it, to him it is sin.

Acts 5:31, AMP

God exalted Him to His right hand to be Prince and Leader and Savior and Deliverer and Preserver, in order to grant repentance to Israel and to bestow forgiveness and release from sins.

Acts 3:19, AMP

So repent (change your mind and purpose); turn around and return [to God], that your sins may be erased (blotted out, wiped clean), that times of refreshing . . . may come from the presence of the Lord.

112. Return to Intimacy

Lord, You are my Father! I may not have turned my back on You, but I now realize I turned my face away. I miss our intimate communication. I miss You and I know You miss me. You are gracious and merciful, Father—You have not forsaken me. I hear Your call to return to the intimacy of our relationship. I heed Your command to acknowledge my guilt. I now confess and forsake my sins to obtain Your mercy. Forgive me, Lord! I am turning back full-faced to You, Father, as I should. Bless me and keep me, Lord. Make your face shine upon mine. Be gracious to me and give me Your peace. I thank You for being abundant in mercy and ready to forgive me when I call upon You. Hear my earnest prayer, O Lord. In the day of my trouble, I am calling upon You. Oh, Father, thank You for the answer to the prayer of faith!

Jeremiah 3:19, NIV

"I thought you would call me 'Father' and not turn away from following me."

Nehemiah 9:17, NKJV

"They refused to obey, and they were not mindful of Your wonders that You did among them. But they hardened their necks, and in their rebellion they appointed a leader to return to their bondage. But You are God, ready to pardon, gracious and merciful, slow to anger, abundant in kindness, and did not forsake them."

Jeremiah 3:12, 13, NIV

" 'Return, faithless Israel,' declares the LORD, 'I will frown on you no longer, for I am merciful,' declares the LORD, 'I will not be angry forever. Only acknowledge your guilt— you have rebelled against the LORD your God . . . and have not obeyed me.' "

Proverbs 28:13, AMP

He who covers his transgressions will not prosper, but whoever confesses and forsakes his sins will obtain mercy.

Numbers 6:24–26, NKJV

" ' "The LORD bless you and keep you; the LORD make His face shine upon you, and be gracious to you; The LORD lift up His countenance upon you, and give you peace." ' "

Psalm 86:5–7, NKJV

For You, Lord, are good, and ready to forgive, and abundant in mercy to all those who call upon You. Give ear, O LORD, to my prayer; and attend to the voice of my supplications. In the day of my trouble I will call upon You, for You will answer me.

113. Revive Me, O Lord

Oh, Father, how did this happen? How did I become careless and calloused about the things that concern You most? I don't want to store up wrath for the day of Your righteous judgment. Cause me to examine my ways and turn back fully to You.

I have stumbled in the sin of self-satisfaction. My priorities are upside down. I have forsaken You as my first love. Forgive me, Lord! Take away my iniquity and receive me graciously, I pray. My soul is laid low. Revive me in keeping with Your Word and Your tender love—according to Your promise. I pray for Your mercy and salvation, that I may rejoice in You again.

Cause me to seek You—in prayer and in the Word—and hear Your voice of unfailing love in the morning. Cause me to know the way in which I should walk. Deliver me from the enemy of my soul. Teach me to do Your will. Lead me in Your ways. Revive me for the sake of Your name and righteousness. Bring my soul out of trouble!

Father, abolish my apathy! Create in me a clean heart and renew a steadfast spirit within me. Do not cast me away from Your presence; do not take Your precious Holy Spirit from me! Restore to me the joy of Your salvation and uphold me by Your Spirit. Then I will share the good news of Your love and mercy with others, and sinners will turn to You for salvation.

Holy and righteous Father, keep Your hand upon me. Revive me. Breathe Your life into me, and I will call upon Your name! Restore me, Lord God Almighty. Cause Your face to shine upon me in favor, and I will be saved!

Romans 2:5, NKJV

In accordance with your hardness and your impenitent heart you are treasuring up for yourself wrath in the day of wrath and revelation of the righteous judgment of God.

Lamentations 3:40, NKJV

Let us search out and examine our ways, and turn back to the LORD.

Proverbs 14:14, NKJV

The backslider in heart will be filled with his own ways, but a good man will be satisfied from above.

Revelation 2:4, NKJV

"I have this against you, that you have left your first love."

Hosea 14:1, 2, NKJV

Return to the LORD your God, for you have stumbled because of your iniquity; take words with you, and return to the LORD. Say to Him, "Take away all iniquity; Receive us graciously, for we will offer the sacrifices of our lips."

Psalm 119:25, NKJV

My soul clings to the dust; revive me according to Your word.

Psalm 119:88, 89, NKJV

Revive me according to Your lovingkindness, So that I may keep the testimony of Your mouth. Forever, O LORD, Your word is settled in heaven.

Psalm 119:40, 41, AMP

Behold, I long for Your precepts; in Your righteousness give me renewed life. Let Your mercy and loving-kindness come also to me, O Lord, even Your salvation according to Your promise.

Psalm 85:6, 7, NKJV

Will You not revive us again, that Your people may rejoice in You? Show us Your mercy, LORD, and grant us Your salvation.

Psalm 143:8–11, NKJV

Cause me to hear Your lovingkindness in the morning, for in You do I trust; cause me to know the way in which I should walk, for I lift up my soul to You. Deliver me, O LORD, from my enemies; in You I take shelter. Teach me to do Your will, for You are my God; Your Spirit is good. Lead me in the land of uprightness. Revive me, O LORD, for Your name's sake! For Your righteousness' sake bring my soul out of trouble.

Psalm 51:10–13, NKJV

Create in me a clean heart, O God, and renew a steadfast spirit within me. Do not cast me away from Your presence, and do not take Your Holy Spirit from me. Restore to me the joy of Your salvation, and uphold me by Your generous Spirit. Then I will teach transgressors Your ways, and sinners shall be converted to You

Psalm 80:17–19, AMP

Let Your hand be upon the man of Your right hand, upon the son of man whom You have made strong for Yourself. Then will we not depart from You; revive us (give us life) and we will call upon Your name. Restore us, O Lord God of hosts; cause Your face to shine [in pleasure, approval, and favor on us], and we shall be saved!

114. Revived Again

I am revived! I returned to God, and He returned to me. My heart was conscience stricken and humbled. God revived my spirit; He breathed new life into me and raised me up from the valley of dry bones.

I am sowing in righteousness, and I will reap in mercy. Through confession and repentance, I plowed up the hardened ground of my heart. Through prayer and the Word, I sought the Lord earnestly. He rained righteousness on me.

God is gracious and merciful to me. He did not turn His face from me when I returned to Him. He saw my headstrong ways, but He loved me freely and healed my backsliding. I am following His leading, and He is restoring comfort to me (and to those who prayed for me). I have returned to Him with my whole heart. God is giving me a heart to know Him through personal experience.

Oh Lord, surely salvation is mine! Your mercy and truth met together at the cruel cross of Calvary, where righteousness and peace kissed. Righteousness goes before You and makes Your footsteps my pathway. Teach me Your way, Lord. Give me an undivided heart. I will praise You forever, for in Your great love You have delivered me from perishing eternally. Cause me continually to put off the old self and put on the nature of Christ. Cause my mind to continually be renewed by Your Word. My heart is confident in You.

I sing Your praises, for Your love and faithfulness toward me are great—reaching to the heavens! Be exalted, O my Lord and my God, be exalted in my life!

Malachi 3:7, NIV

"Ever since the time of your forefathers you have turned away from my decrees and have not kept them. Return to me, and I will return to you," says the LORD Almighty.

Isaiah 57:15, AMP

Thus says the high and lofty One—He who inhabits eternity, whose name is Holy: I dwell in the high and holy place, but with him also who is of a thoroughly penitent and humble spirit, to revive the spirit of the humble and to revive the heart of the thoroughly penitent [bruised with sorrow for sin].

Ezekiel 37:4, 5, AMP

O you dry bones, hear the word of the Lord. Thus says the Lord God to these bones: Behold, I will cause breath and spirit to enter you, and you shall live.

Hosea 10:12, NKJV

Sow for yourselves righteousness; reap in mercy; break up your fallow ground, for it is time to seek the LORD, till He comes and rains righteousness on you.

2 Chronicles 30:9, NKJV

"The LORD your God is gracious and merciful, and will not turn His face from you if you return to Him."

Isaiah 57:18, AMP

I have seen his [willful] ways, but I will heal him; I will lead him also and will recompense him and restore comfort to him and to those who mourn for him.

Hosea 14:4, NKJV

"I will heal their backsliding, I will love them freely, for My anger has turned away from him."

Jeremiah 24:7, AMP

I will give them a heart to know (recognize, understand, and be acquainted with) Me, that I am the Lord; and they will be My people, and I will be their God, for they will return to Me with their whole heart.

Psalm 85:9–13, NKJV

Surely His salvation is near to those who fear Him. . . . Mercy and truth have met together; righteousness and peace have kissed each other. Truth shall spring out of the earth, and righteousness shall look down from heaven. Yes, the LORD will give what is good. . . . Righteousness will go before Him, and shall make His footsteps our pathway.

Psalm 86:11–13, NIV

Teach me your way, O LORD, and I will walk in your truth; give me an undivided heart, that I may fear your name. I will praise you, O Lord my God, with all my heart; I will glorify your name forever. For great is your love toward me; you have delivered me from the depths of the grave.

Ephesians 4:22–24, AMP

Strip yourselves of your former nature [put off and discard your old unrenewed self] which characterized your previous manner of life and becomes corrupt through lusts and desires that spring from delusion; and be constantly renewed in the spirit of your mind [having a fresh mental and spiritual attitude], and put on the new nature (the regenerate self) created in God's image, [Godlike] in true righteousness and holiness.

Psalm 57:7, 10, AMP

My heart is fixed, O God, my heart is steadfast and confident! I will sing and make melody . . . For Your mercy and loving-kindness are great, reaching to the heavens, and Your truth and faithfulness to the clouds.

115. Righteousness by Faith

I am the righteousness of God in Christ Jesus. God has **imputed** (credited) Christ's righteousness to me. Righteousness by faith is the only righteousness that exists.

Christ's robe of righteousness does not cover sin that I refuse to confess and forsake. God also **imparts** Christ's righteousness to me. He fills me with His righteousness, which develops Christ's character in me and causes me to conduct myself according to God's right way of doing things.

Therefore, I take heed to avoid the risk of thinking I stand firm when I am really on shaky ground. I pay attention to my conduct to ensure I am not fooling myself. I take a daily spiritual inventory to make certain that I do not become disqualified. Having been made righteous, I now put it into practice by following God's way of thinking and acting. I am obeying His commandments by His righteousness within me.

By His abundance of grace and the gift of righteousness, I reign in life through Christ.

The fruit of righteousness in my life is peace. The result righteousness has in my heart is a calm assurance forever.

2 Corinthians 5:21, NIV

God made him who had no sin to be sin for us, so that in him we might become the **righteousness** of God.

1 Corinthians 1:30, AMP

But it is from Him that you have your life **in Christ Jesus,** Whom God made . . . **our Righteousness** [thus making us upright and putting us in right standing with God].

Romans 9:30, NKJV

Gentiles, who did not pursue righteousness, have attained to righteousness, even the righteousness of faith.

Isaiah 64:6, NKJV

We are all like an unclean thing, and all our righteousnesses are like filthy rags.

Jeremiah 23:6, NKJV

"Now this is His name . . . **THE LORD OUR RIGHTEOUSNESS.**"

Psalm 23:3, NKJV

He restores my soul; He leads me in the paths of righteousness for His name's sake.

Isaiah 61:10, NKJV

My soul shall be joyful in my God; for He has clothed me with the garments of salvation, He has covered me with the robe of righteousness.

1 Corinthians 10:12, NKJV

Let him who thinks he stands take heed lest he fall.

1 Corinthians 9:27, NKJV

I discipline my body and bring it into subjection, lest, when I have preached to others, I myself should become disqualified.

1 John 2:29, NKJV

If you know that He is righteous, you know that everyone who practices righteousness is born of Him.

Psalm 85:13, NKJV

Righteousness will go before Him, and shall make His footsteps our pathway.

1 John 3:7, 8, NKJV

Little children, let no one deceive you. **He who practices righteousness is righteous, just as He is righteous.** He who sins is of the devil. . . . For this purpose the Son of God was manifested, that He might destroy the works of the devil.

Romans 5:17, NKJV

Those who receive abundance of grace and of the gift of righteousness will reign in life through the One, Jesus Christ.

Isaiah 32:17, NKJV

The work of righteousness will be peace, and the effect of righteousness, quietness and assurance forever.

116. Rooted in Righteousness

Christ dwells in my heart through faith and through the power of His Spirit within me. I am rooted and grounded in His love. I have implanted His Word within my heart, and it has taken root.

As the transforming power of His Word grows within me, it saves my soul. I do not deceive myself by merely listening, but rather I put His Word into practice. I revere and worship God and keep His commandments—this is His purpose for me and is the root of my godly character.

When persecution arises because of the Word, I do not fall away. My deep roots in His love and His Word make it possible for me to stand firm in faith. Nothing can uproot me—not even the enemy of my soul who roars against me like a hungry lion.

I have received the anointing of the Holy Spirit, and He keeps me firmly rooted in Christ. My deep roots cause me to yield good fruit—to do good works in the Lord. I have received an abundance of grace and the gift of righteousness. Rooted in Christ, I am rooted in righteousness. I reign in life through Him.

Ephesians 3:16–19, NKJV

That He would grant you, according to the riches of His glory, to be strengthened with might through His Spirit in the inner man, that Christ may dwell in your hearts through faith; that you, being rooted and grounded in love, may be able to comprehend with all the saints what is the width and length and depth and height—to know the love of Christ which passes knowledge; that you may be filled with all the fullness of God.

James 1:21, 22, AMP

Get rid of all uncleanness and the rampant outgrowth of wickedness, and in a humble (gentle, modest) spirit receive and welcome the Word which implanted and rooted [in your hearts] contains the power to save your souls. But be doers of the Word [obey the message], and not merely listeners to it, betraying yourselves [into deception by reasoning contrary to the truth].

Ecclesiastes 12:13, AMP

All has been heard; the end of the matter is: Fear God [revere and worship Him, knowing that He is] and keep His commandments, for this is the whole of man [the full, original purpose of his creation, the object of God's providence, the root of character, the foundation of all happiness, the adjustment to all inharmonious circumstances and conditions under the sun] and the whole [duty] for every man.

Mark 4:17, AMP

They have no real root in themselves, and so they endure for a little while; then when trouble or persecution arises on account of the Word, they immediately are offended (become displeased, indignant, resentful) and they stumble and fall away.

Proverbs 12:3, NIV

The righteous cannot be uprooted.

1 Peter 5:8, 9, AMP

Be well balanced (temperate, sober of mind), be vigilant and cautious at all times; for that enemy of yours, the devil, roams around like a lion roaring [in fierce hunger], seeking someone to seize upon and devour. Withstand him; be firm in faith [against his onset—rooted, established, strong, immovable, and determined], knowing that the same (identical) sufferings are appointed to your brotherhood (the whole body of Christians) throughout the world.

1 John 2:27, AMP

But as for you, the anointing (the sacred appointment, the unction) which you received from Him abides [permanently] in you; [so] then you have no need that anyone should instruct you. But just as His anointing teaches you concerning everything and is true and is no falsehood, so you must abide in (live in, never depart from) Him [being rooted in Him, knit to Him], just as [His anointing] has taught you [to do].

Proverbs 12:12, NKJV

The root of the righteous yields fruit.

Romans 5:17, NKJV

Those who receive abundance of grace and of the gift of righteousness will reign in life through the One, Jesus Christ.

117. Running the Race of Faith

By God's grace, I will run well the race of faith. I allow no one and nothing to hinder me from obeying God's truth. I lay down frivolous activities that slow and impede my progress, and I set aside those "ball and chain" sins that ensnare my feet and cause me to stumble. With my eyes fixed on Jesus, I run to Him, eager to meet Him face-to-face.

I am running this race to lay hold of the prize God has reserved for me in heaven. An athlete denies himself everything that would prevent him from doing his best just to win a wreath that withers. I conduct myself temperately to be crowned with eternal blessedness that cannot wither. I have this purpose in mind with every step. I am not shadowboxing; I have a real adversary. I take my training seriously so that I will not become unfit and unable to finish the race.

I run in God's strength, as He works in me to will and to act according to His delight.

Galatians 5:7, 8, NASB

You were running well; who hindered you from obeying the truth? This persuasion did not come from Him who calls you.

Hebrews 12:1, 2, NKJV

We also, since we are surrounded by so great a cloud of witnesses, let us lay aside every weight, and the sin which so easily ensnares us, and let us run with endurance the race that is set before us, looking unto Jesus, the author and finisher of our faith.

1 Corinthians 9:24–27, AMP

Do you not know that in a race all the runners compete, but [only] one receives the prize? So run [your race] that you may lay hold [of the prize] and make it yours. Now every athlete who goes into training conducts himself temperately and restricts himself in all things. They do it to win a wreath that will soon wither, but we [do it to receive a crown of eternal blessedness] that cannot wither. Therefore I do not run uncertainly (without definite aim), I do not box like one beating the air and striking without an adversary. But [like a boxer] I buffet my body [handle it roughly, discipline it by hardships] and subdue it, for fear that after proclaiming to others the Gospel and things pertaining to it, I myself should become unfit [not stand the test, be unapproved and rejected as a counterfeit].

Philippians 2:13, AMP

[Not in your own strength] for it is God Who is all the while effectually at work in you [energizing and creating in you the power and desire], both to will and to work for His good pleasure and satisfaction and delight.

118. Sanctified by God

God's will is that I be sanctified—made holy, and set apart for His special purposes. I am sanctified by faith in Christ Jesus; He is my sanctification. I am sanctified through His once-for-all sacrifice and His blood of the eternal covenant. I am sanctified by the God of peace and His Word. I am sanctified by the Holy Spirit, for the purpose of obedience to Christ and eternal life.

1 Thessalonians 4:3, NASB

This is the will of God, your sanctification.

Acts 26:18, NKJV

That they may receive forgiveness of sins and an inheritance among those who are sanctified by faith in Me.

1 Corinthians 1:30, NKJV

Of Him you are in Christ Jesus, who became for us . . . sanctification.

Hebrews 10:10, NASB

We have been sanctified through the offering of the body of Jesus Christ once for all.

Hebrews 13:12, NASB

Jesus also, that He might sanctify the people through His own blood, suffered outside the gate.

1 Thessalonians 5:23, NKJV

Now may the God of peace Himself sanctify you completely; and may your whole spirit, soul, and body be preserved blameless at the coming of our Lord Jesus Christ.

John 17:17, NIV

"Sanctify them by the truth; your word is truth."

Ephesians 5:26, NKJV

That He might sanctify and cleanse it with the washing of water by the word.

1 Peter 1:2, NIV

Who have been chosen according to the foreknowledge of God the Father, through the sanctifying work of the Spirit, for obedience to Jesus Christ and sprinkling by his blood.

119. Satan's Schemes

I am alert, watching out for the enemy of my soul. I am aware of Satan's schemes and devices. He always tries to get me to doubt and disobey God's Word. I am not fooled when Satan masquerades as an angel of light. He packages sin to be pleasurable for a season. Sin is nothing more than gift-wrapped garbage—filth cloaked in deceit to entice Satan's victims, but which ultimately leads to misery, regret, and death.

I take the escape route God provides me to avoid temptation. I submit my life to His control and, then, as I resist the devil, he must flee.

1 Peter 5:8, NKJV

Be sober, be vigilant; because your adversary the devil walks about like a roaring lion, seeking whom he may devour.

2 Corinthians 2:11, AMP

To keep Satan from getting the advantage over us; for we are not ignorant of his wiles and intentions.

Genesis 3:1, AMP

Now the serpent was more subtle and crafty. . . . And he [Satan] said to the woman, Can it really be that God has said, You shall not eat from every tree of the garden?

2 Corinthians 11:14, 15, AMP

Satan himself masquerades as an angel of light; so it is not surprising if his servants also masquerade as ministers of righteousness.

James 1:14, 15, AMP

Every person is tempted when he is drawn away, enticed and baited by his own evil desire (lusts, passions). Then the evil desire, when it has conceived, gives birth to sin, and sin, when it is fully matured, brings forth death.

1 Corinthians 10:13, NIV

No temptation has seized you except what is common to man. And God is faithful; he will not let you be tempted beyond what you can bear. But when you are tempted, he will also provide a way out so that you can stand up under it.

James 4:7, NASB

Submit therefore to God. Resist the devil and he will flee from you.

120. Sealed for the Day of Redemption

I am included "in Christ." In Christ, I am sealed for the day of redemption. Because I remain in Christ (not turning away from Him), absolutely nothing can separate me from the abundant love that God has for me!

I walk hand-in-hand with my Lord. He will not let my foot slip. No one can snatch me from His hand! I find complete security in Christ. I will not turn away from Him! I have died to sin, and my true life is hidden with Christ (locked safely in Him).

Ephesians 1:13, 14, NIV

You also were included in Christ when you heard the word of truth, the gospel of your salvation. Having believed, **you were marked in him with a seal, the promised Holy Spirit,** who is a deposit guaranteeing our inheritance until the redemption of those who are God's possession—to the praise of his glory.

Ephesians 4:30, AMP

Do not grieve the Holy Spirit of God [do not offend or vex or sadden Him], by Whom **you were sealed** (marked, branded as God's own, secured) **for the day of redemption** (of final deliverance through Christ from evil and the consequences of sin).

Romans 8:38, 39, NKJV

I am persuaded that neither death nor life, nor angels nor principalities nor powers, nor things present nor things to come, nor height nor depth, nor any other created thing, shall be able to separate us from the love of God which is in Christ Jesus our Lord.

Psalm 121:3, AMP

He will not allow your foot to slip or to be moved; He Who keeps you will not slumber.

John 10:27–30, NKJV

"My sheep hear My voice, and I know them, and they follow Me. And I give them eternal life, and they shall never perish; neither shall anyone snatch them out of My hand. My Father, who has given them to Me, is greater than all; and no one is able to snatch them out of My Father's hand. I and My Father are one."

Colossians 3:3, NIV

You died, and your life is now hidden with Christ in God.

121. Search Me and Show Me Where I Fall Short

Holy and righteous Father, please search my heart and mind. Show me the areas in which I fall short of Your glory. Please lead me to godly sorrow and repentance. Please wash me thoroughly and repeatedly in the precious blood of Jesus and cleanse me of my sin.

I want to know Jesus Christ and the power of His resurrection. I want to be more like Jesus. Create in me a pure heart and consistent actions of faith. I rely on Your power to be made perfect in my weakness.

Psalm 139:23, 24, NIV

Search me, O God, and know my heart; test me and know my anxious thoughts. See if there is any offensive way in me, and lead me in the way everlasting.

Psalm 19:12, AMP

Clear me from hidden [and unconscious] faults.

Romans 3:23, 24, NKJV

All have sinned and fall short of the glory of God, being justified freely by His grace through the redemption that is in Christ Jesus.

2 Corinthians 7:10, NIV

Godly sorrow brings repentance that leads to salvation and leaves no regret.

Psalm 51:2, AMP

Wash me thoroughly [and repeatedly] from my iniquity and guilt and cleanse me and make me wholly pure from my sin.

1 John 1:7, NKJV

If we walk in the light as He is in the light, we have fellowship with one another, and the blood of Jesus Christ His Son cleanses us from all sin.

Philippians 3:10, NIV

I want to know Christ and the power of his resurrection.

2 Corinthians 12:9, NIV

He said to me, "My grace is sufficient for you, for my power is made perfect in weakness."

122. Seek First His Kingdom and His Righteousness

My first priority in life is to **do all things** according to God's will. I seek Him first and gain understanding of the right way to think and to do all things. In the morning, I lay my requests before Him and wait expectantly for His response. He teaches me His will. I lean on what His Word says, rather than on my own limited understanding. He directs my steps in His glorious path of life, and I find joy walking in His presence.

Matthew 6:31–34, AMP

Do not worry and be anxious, saying, What are we going to have to eat? or, What are we going to have to drink? or, What are we going to have to wear? . . . . Your heavenly Father knows well that you need them all. **But seek (aim at and strive after) first of all His kingdom and His righteousness (His way of doing and being right),** and then all these things taken together will be given you besides. So do not worry or be anxious about tomorrow, for tomorrow will have worries and anxieties of its own. Sufficient for each day is its own trouble.

Psalm 5:3, NIV

In the morning, O LORD, you hear my voice; in the morning I lay my requests before you and wait in expectation.

Psalm 143:8–10, NKJV

Cause me to hear Your lovingkindness in the morning, for in You do I trust; cause me to know the way in which I should walk, for I lift up my soul to You. . . . Teach me to do Your will, for You are my God; Your Spirit is good. Lead me in the land of uprightness.

Proverbs 3:5, 6, NKJV

Trust in the LORD with all your heart, and lean not on your own understanding; in all your ways acknowledge Him, and He shall direct your paths.

Psalm 16:11, AMP

You will show me the path of life; in Your presence is fullness of joy.

123. Seek His Face

Abba, Father, I am seeking Your face. I am seeking You with all of my heart and soul, clinging to the promise that I will come to know You. My Father, cause me to seek Your face and not Your hand. I want to know You—to understand Your love and holiness, to experience Your presence. Cause my first priority in life to be seeking You. Lead me in your way of truth. Then I know You will show Yourself strong on my behalf and continue to prosper me in every way. I trust You, Lord, for You never forsake those who seek You.

Psalm 105:4, NASB

Seek the Lord and His strength; seek His face continually.

Psalm 27:8, NKJV

When You said, "Seek My face," my heart said to You, "Your face, Lord, I will seek."

Deuteronomy 4:29, NKJV

"From there you will seek the Lord your God, and you will find Him if you seek Him with all your heart and with all your soul."

John 17:3, NASB

"This is eternal life, that they may know You, the only true God, and Jesus Christ whom You have sent."

Matthew 6:33, NKJV

"Seek first the kingdom of God and His righteousness, and all these things shall be added to you."

1 Chronicles 28:9, NKJV

"The Lord searches all hearts and understands all the intent of the thoughts. If you seek Him, He will be found by you; but if you forsake Him, He will cast you off forever."

2 Chronicles 26:5, NASB

He continued to seek God . . . and as long as he sought the Lord, God prospered him.

Psalm 9:10, NIV

Those who know your name will trust in you, for you, Lord, have never forsaken those who seek you.

124. Sharing in Christ's Sufferings

Lord, I will count it a privilege to share in Christ's suffering, just as I will also share in His inheritance. My suffering is temporary and cannot compare with those things You have in store for me. I will follow in Christ's footsteps, that I may know Him better and the power of His resurrection and the fellowship of His sufferings. When cursed, I will bless; when persecuted, I will endure; when slandered, I will answer kindly. When I am insulted because of the name of Christ, I will remember that I am blessed—for Your Spirit rests on me. You are the God of all grace. I will rejoice in my suffering, because I know that after I have suffered a little while, You will establish me in Your strength.

Philippians 1:29, AMP

You have been granted [the privilege] for Christ's sake not only to believe in (adhere to, rely on, and trust in) Him, but also to suffer in His behalf.

Romans 8:17, 18, AMP

If we are [His] children, then we are [His] heirs also: heirs of God and fellow heirs with Christ [sharing His inheritance with Him]; only we must share His suffering if we are to share His glory. [But what of that?] For I consider that the sufferings of this present time (this present life) are not worth being compared with the glory that is about to be revealed to us and in us and for us and conferred on us!

2 Corinthians 4:16, 17, NKJV

We do not lose heart. Even though our outward man is perishing, yet the inward man is being renewed day by day. For our light affliction, which is but for a moment, is working for us a far more exceeding and eternal weight of glory.

Philippians 3:10, NKJV

That I may know Him and the power of His resurrection, and the fellowship of His sufferings, being conformed to His death.

1 Corinthians 4:12, 13, NIV

When we are cursed, we bless; when we are persecuted, we endure it; when we are slandered, we answer kindly.

1 Peter 5:10, NASB

After you have suffered for a little while, the God of all grace, who called you to His eternal glory in Christ, will Himself perfect, confirm, strengthen and establish you.

125. Speak From a Heart of Love

If I have all knowledge and do not speak from a heart gripped by the Lord's love, I am nothing more than a noisy, clanging cymbal before God and man. By God's grace, I always speak from a heart of love and not a "head of knowledge." Head knowledge can "puff" me up, but speaking the truth in love will always build others up in Christ Jesus. God gives me the words to speak to those who are wearied from life's battles.

When confronted by someone who distorts God's Word or resists the truths of Scripture, I am careful to act in love and to be gentle and patient in my instruction. I know that except for the grace of God, I would be just like them. I pray for God to lead them to greater understanding and acceptance of His truths. I pray He will open their hearts and lead them to repentance. I pray for God to make me faithful to Him by my intercessory prayers for those He has led into my path, and to help me instruct them in the good and right way.

1 Corinthians 13:1, NASB

If I speak with the tongues of men and of angels, but do not have love, I have become a noisy gong or a clanging cymbal.

Ephesians 4:15, NIV

Speaking the truth in love, we will in all things grow up into him who is the Head, that is, Christ.

1 Corinthians 8:1, NIV

We know that we all possess knowledge. Knowledge puffs up, but love builds up.

Isaiah 50:4, NKJV

"The Lord God has given me the tongue of the learned, that I should know how to speak a word in season to him who is weary."

2 Timothy 2:24, 25, NIV

The Lord's servant must not quarrel. . . . Those who oppose him he must gently instruct, in the hope that God will grant them repentance leading them to a knowledge of the truth.

1 Samuel 12:23, AMP

Moreover, as for me, far be it from me that I should sin against the Lord by ceasing to pray for you; but I will instruct you in the good and right way.

126. The Spirit of Power and Self-discipline Is Mine

The Holy Spirit of God lives in me. I have been given a spirit of power, love, and holiness. I have been given a spirit of self-discipline and peace. I have surrendered control of my life to the Spirit of God. Hallelujah, God has cut me free from the cord of the wicked that tried to bind me.

I am dead to sin, but alive to God. I am under the power of His grace, and sin shall not be my master. I have put on Christ Jesus, and I make no provision for my flesh.

God gives me victory through my Lord Jesus Christ.

Romans 8:9, NIV

You, however, are controlled not by the sinful nature but by the Spirit, if the Spirit of God lives in you. And if anyone does not have the Spirit of Christ, he does not belong to Christ.

2 Timothy 1:7, NIV

For God did not give us a spirit of timidity, but a spirit of power, of love and of self-discipline.

1 Corinthians 14:33, NKJV

God is not the author of confusion but of peace

Psalm 129:4, NIV

The LORD is righteous; he has cut me free from the cords of the wicked.

1 John 3:8, NKJV

For this purpose the Son of God was manifested, that He might destroy the works of the devil.

Romans 6:11–14, NKJV

You also, reckon yourselves to be dead indeed to sin, but alive to God in Christ Jesus our Lord. For sin shall not have dominion over you, for you are not under law but under grace.

Romans 13:14, NKJV

Put on the Lord Jesus Christ, and make no provision for the flesh.

1 Corinthians 15:57, NIV

Thanks be to God! He gives us the victory through our Lord Jesus Christ.

127. Triumph Over Temptation

I am an overcomer! I overcome evil with good. God is faithful; He gives me strength to triumph over every temptation. I can stand faithful to Him under the weight of any temptation. I am never tempted beyond what I can bear. My heavenly Father always provides me with an escape route from evil.

He is my "hiding place." I dwell in the secret place of the Most High. He preserves me from trouble and surrounds me with songs of deliverance. God guides me by His Word. I depend upon Him to deliver me from every evil attack and bring me safely into His heavenly kingdom, receiving me to glory.

It is God Himself who will sanctify me completely, making me holy. He calls me to holiness, and He who calls me is faithful. If I simply surrender control of my life to His loving power, He will keep me blameless at the coming of my Lord Jesus Christ.

Romans 12:21, NIV

Do not be overcome by evil, but overcome evil with good.

1 Corinthians 10:13, NASB

No temptation has overtaken you but such as is common to man; and God is faithful, who will not allow you to be tempted beyond what you are able, but with the temptation will provide the way of escape also, so that you will be able to endure it.

Psalm 32:7, NASB

You are my hiding place; You preserve me from trouble; You surround me with songs of deliverance.

Psalm 91:1, NKJV

He who dwells in the secret place of the Most High shall abide under the shadow of the Almighty.

2 Timothy 4:18, NIV

The Lord will rescue me from every evil attack and will bring me safely to his heavenly kingdom. To him be glory for ever and ever.

1 Thessalonians 5:23, 24, NASB

Now may the God of peace Himself sanctify you entirely; and may your spirit and soul and body be preserved complete, without blame at the coming of our Lord Jesus Christ. Faithful is He who calls you, and He also will bring it to pass.

128. Two-Edged-Sword Authority

God has given me the authority and eternal power of His word. His word is alive, active, immovable, and unshakable. His word is a two-edged sword—

The first edge struck when He spoke it.

The second edge strikes when I speak it.

As I speak the word, I hear the voice of the Lord. I am returning His word to Him, and His word does not return void, but accomplishes every purpose for which He sent it. He actively watches over His word to make certain it is fulfilled at the perfect time which He has appointed.

Hebrews 4:12, NKJV

The word of God is **living and powerful**, and sharper than any two-edged sword, piercing even to the division of soul and spirit, and of joints and marrow, and is a discerner of the thoughts and intents of the heart.

Isaiah 55:9–13, NIV

"As the heavens are higher than the earth, so are my ways higher than your ways and my thoughts than your thoughts. As the rain and the snow come down from heaven, and do not return to it without watering the earth and making it bud and flourish, so that it yields seed for the sower and bread for the eater, **so is my word that goes out from my mouth: It will not return to me empty, but will accomplish what I desire and achieve the purpose for which I sent it. . . .** This will be for the LORD's renown, for an everlasting sign, which will not be destroyed."

Jeremiah 1:12, AMP

Then said the Lord to me, You have seen well, for I am alert and active, **watching over My word to perform it.**

Luke 1:20, AMP

But My words are of a kind which will be fulfilled in the appointed and proper time.

Habakkuk 2:3, AMP

The vision is yet for **an appointed time** and it hastens to the end [fulfillment]; it will not deceive or disappoint. Though it tarry, wait [earnestly] for it, because it will surely come; it will not be behindhand on its appointed day.

129. An Unquenchable Desire for God's Word

I have an unquenchable desire for the inexhaustible word of God. As a disciple of Jesus Christ, the Messiah, I live in (and according to) His word. Because I adhere to His teachings, I have an intimate knowledge (through personal experience) of the truth—and—His truth has set me free!

Psalm 42:1, 2, NIV

As the deer pants for streams of water, so my soul pants for you, O God. My soul thirsts for God, for the living God. When can I go and meet with God?

Jeremiah 15:16, NKJV

Your words were found, and I ate them, and Your word was to me the joy and rejoicing of my heart; for I am called by Your name, O LORD God of hosts.

Psalm 119:103, NKJV

How sweet are Your words to my taste, sweeter than honey to my mouth!

Job 23:12, NKJV

I have not departed from the commandment of His lips; **I have treasured the words of His mouth more than my necessary food.**

Matthew 4:4, NKJV

"It is written, 'Man shall not live by bread alone, but by every word that proceeds from the mouth of God.' "

Psalm 119:11, NKJV

Your word I have hidden in my heart, that I might not sin against You.

John 8:31, 32, AMP

So Jesus said . . . **If you abide in My word [hold fast to My teachings and live in accordance with them], you are truly My disciples.** And you will know the Truth, and the Truth will set you free.

John 8:36, NIV

"If the Son sets you free, you will be free indeed."

130. Walking As Children of Light

I walk in the light of God's Word, and the blood of Jesus Christ cleanses me from all sin. By the power of His grace, I shun evil. He has taught me to hate the darkness of evil and to grip firmly what is good. I demonstrate my fear—my reverent awe and respect— for God in this way. Therefore, His eyes are upon me, and His ears are open to my prayer!

I do not follow a crowd to pursue the immoral ways of the world. To be friends with the world's system is to be an enemy of God. All the ways of the world—the lust of the flesh, the lust of the eyes, and the pride of life—are not of God.

Bad company corrupts good morals. I will not intentionally unite myself with an unbeliever in a binding personal relationship or business partnership. I come out from among them and take my stand separately for the Lord. I avoid sexual immorality, impure activity, covetous desire, and greedy attitudes—for it is because of these worldly dealings that God's wrath will come upon the disobedient.

I walk as an obedient child of God—a child of light! Following after Jesus Christ, my Lord, I have the light of life! He causes my path to shine brighter every day.

Psalm 119:105, NASB

Your word is a lamp to my feet and a light to my path.

Psalm 119:130, NKJV

The entrance of Your words gives light; it gives understanding to the simple.

1 John 1:6, 7, NKJV

If we say that we have fellowship with Him, and walk in darkness, we lie and do not practice the truth. But if we walk in the light as He is in the light, we have fellowship with one another, and the blood of Jesus Christ His Son cleanses us from all sin.

Proverbs 8:13, NIV

To fear the LORD is to hate evil.

Romans 12:9, AMP

Hate what is evil [loathe all ungodliness, turn in horror from wickedness], but hold fast to that which is good.

1 Peter 3:12, NIV

"The eyes of the Lord are on the righteous and his ears are attentive to their prayer, but the face of the Lord is against those who do evil."

Exodus 23:2, AMP

You shall not follow a crowd to do evil.

James 4:4, AMP

Do you not know that being the world's friend is being God's enemy? So whoever chooses to be a friend of the world takes his stand as an enemy of God.

1 John 2:16, NKJV

All that is in the world—the lust of the flesh, the lust of the eyes, and the pride of life—is not of the Father but is of the world.

1 Corinthians 15:33, NASB

Do not be deceived: "Bad company corrupts good morals."

2 Corinthians 6:14, AMP

Do not be unequally yoked with unbelievers [do not make mismated alliances with them or come under a different yoke with them, inconsistent with your faith]. For what partnership have right living and right standing with God with iniquity and lawlessness? Or how can light have fellowship with darkness?

2 Corinthians 6:17, NIV

"Therefore come out from them and be separate, says the Lord. Touch no unclean thing, and I will receive you."

Ephesians 5:5–8, NKJV

This you know, that no fornicator, unclean person, nor covetous man, who is an idolater, has any inheritance in the kingdom of Christ and God. Let no one deceive you with empty words, for because of these things the wrath of God comes upon the sons of disobedience. Therefore do not be partakers with them. For you were once darkness, but now you are light in the Lord. Walk as children of light.

John 8:12, NASB

"I am the Light of the world; he who follows Me will not walk in the darkness, but will have the Light of life."

Proverbs 4:18, NKJV

The path of the just is like the shining sun, that shines ever brighter unto the perfect day.

131. Walking in Christ's Footsteps

I am walking in Christ's footsteps. His word is a lamp unto my feet and illuminates my path to show me the direction of my future steps.

He sustains me with His powerful word, and causes me to walk as He did.

Psalm 119:105, AMP

Your word is a lamp to my feet and a light to my path.

Proverbs 4:18, NKJV

The path of the just is like the shining sun, that shines ever brighter unto the perfect day.

Colossians 2:6, AMP

As you have therefore received Christ, . . . walk (regulate your lives and conduct yourselves) in union with and conformity to Him.

2 John 1:6, NIV

This is love: that we walk in obedience to his commands. . . . His command is that you walk in love.

John 8:12, NIV

When Jesus spoke again to the people, he said, "I am the light of the world. Whoever follows me will never walk in darkness, but will have the light of life."

Psalm 89:15, NIV

Blessed are those who have learned to acclaim you, who walk in the light of your presence, O Lord.

Psalm 85:13, NKJV

Righteousness will go before Him, and shall make His footsteps our pathway.

Hebrews 1:3, AMP

He [Jesus] is the sole expression of the glory of God [the Light-being, the out-raying or radiance of the divine], and He is the perfect imprint and very image of [God's] nature, **upholding and maintaining and guiding and propelling the universe by His mighty word of power.**

1 John 2:6, NIV

Whoever claims to live in him must walk as Jesus did.

132. Walking in the Power of God's Spirit

I am walking in the power of God's Spirit. Everything my Father requires of me, He empowers me to accomplish. He continues to equip me and strengthen me.

As I cooperate with Him, He works in me to desire His will and to do His will. I trust Him to **cause** me to be all that He has **called** me to be. I can't perfect my walk by my flesh—I need His power to over come my weakness. I start with the Spirit and continue by the Spirit. I will not deny the Spirit's power.

Ephesians 3:16, NIV

I pray that out of his glorious riches he may strengthen you with power through his Spirit in your inner being.

Hebrews 13:20, 21, NIV

May the God of peace . . . equip you with everything good for doing his will, and may he work in us what is pleasing to him, through Jesus Christ.

Philippians 2:12, 13, NKJV

Therefore, my beloved, as you have always obeyed, . . . work out your own salvation with fear and trembling; for it is God who works in you both to will and to do for His good pleasure.

Galatians 3:3, NKJV

Are you so foolish? Having begun in the Spirit, are you now being made perfect by the flesh?

2 Corinthians 12:9, NIV

"My grace is sufficient for you, for my power is made perfect in weakness."

Philippians 4:13, AMP

I have strength for all things in Christ Who empowers me.

2 Timothy 3:1–5, NIV

There will be terrible times in the last days. People will be lovers of themselves, lovers of money, boastful, proud, abusive, disobedient to their parents, ungrateful, unholy, without love, unforgiving, slanderous, without self-control, brutal, not lovers of the good, treacherous, rash, conceited, lovers of pleasure rather than lovers of God—having a form of godliness but denying its power. Have nothing to do with them.

133. Walking in Step With the Spirit

I will not exchange eternal salvation for worldly gains. I choose daily to pick up my cross! Through the power of the Holy Spirit, I willingly crucify my sinful nature, denying selfishness. In this way, I find the higher life.

As a child of God, I am guided throughout the day by the Holy Spirit. Father, please teach me to do Your will! Help me to walk in step with Your Holy Spirit—not lagging behind, nor running ahead.

Matthew 16:26, 27, NIV

"What good will it be for a man if he gains the whole world, yet forfeits his soul? Or what can a man give in exchange for his soul? For the Son of Man is going to come in his Father's glory with his angels, and then he will reward each person according to what he has done."

Luke 9:23, NKJV

Then He said to them all, "If anyone desires to come after Me, let him deny himself, and take up his cross daily, and follow Me."

Romans 8:13, 14, NIV

If you live according to the sinful nature, you will die; **but if by the Spirit you put to death the misdeeds of the body, you will live,** because those who are led by the Spirit of God are sons of God.

Matthew 10:38, 39, AMP

He who does not take up his cross and follow Me . . . is not worthy of Me. Whoever finds his [lower] life will lose it [the higher life], and whoever loses his [lower] life on My account will find it [the higher life].

Psalm 143:10, AMP

Teach me to do Your will, for You are my God; let Your good Spirit lead me into a level country and into the land of uprightness.

Galatians 5:24, 25, AMP

And those who belong to Christ Jesus (the Messiah) have **crucified the flesh (the godless human nature)** with its passions and appetites and desires. **If we live by the [Holy] Spirit, let us also walk by the Spirit.** [If by the Holy Spirit we have our life in God, let us go forward walking in line, our conduct controlled by the Spirit.]

134. Weapons of Spiritual Power

The devil's destructive forces of darkness and evil are waging a war against the Lord's creative power of light and purity. The greatest battleground is in my mind! God knows I can't confront this spiritual struggle using human methods, so He supplies me with spiritual weapons of divine power—His Word, His Spirit, His gospel of truth and salvation, Christ's righteousness, faith, and prayer.

I put on the whole armor of God and stand with my feet firmly planted on the Rock of my salvation. With His weapons and by His power, I squash speculations that oppose His truths, I shatter strongholds of the devil, and I seize my thoughts—making them obedient to Christ.

Submitting to God, I resist the devil. The devil flees as I draw near to God and God draws near to me. The Lord is righteous; He cuts me free from the cords of the wicked that try to bind me.

Ephesians 6:12, NIV

For our struggle is not against flesh and blood, but against the rulers, against the authorities, against the powers of this dark world and against the spiritual forces of evil in the heavenly realms.

2 Corinthians 10:3–5, NIV

Though we live in the world, we do not wage war as the world does. The weapons we fight with are not the weapons of the world. On the contrary, they have divine power to demolish strongholds. We demolish arguments and every pretension that sets itself up against the knowledge of God, and we take captive every thought to make it obedient to Christ.

Ephesians 6:13, NASB

Therefore, take up the full armor of God, so that you will be able to resist in the evil day, and having done everything, to stand firm.

James 4:7, 8, NKJV

Therefore submit to God. Resist the devil and he will flee from you. Draw near to God and He will draw near to you. Cleanse your hands, you sinners; and purify your hearts, you double-minded.

Psalm 129:4, NIV

The LORD is righteous; he has cut me free from the cords of the wicked.

135. Wisdom From God

Jesus is the Wisdom of God. I keep asking for—and God keeps giving me—wisdom and prudence through Jesus Christ. His counsel and sound judgment are mine, through His powerful word and the understanding given to me by the Holy Spirit. He causes me to understand the testimony of God by the mind of Christ. With wisdom from above, I am coming to know my Lord and to understand more fully His loving plan for my life.

1 Corinthians 1:30, AMP

It is from Him that you have your life in Christ Jesus, Whom God made our Wisdom from God, . . . our Righteousness [thus making us upright and putting us in right standing with God], and our Consecration [making us pure and holy], and our Redemption [providing our ransom from eternal penalty for sin].

James 1:5, NKJV

If any of you lacks wisdom, let him ask of God, who gives to all liberally and without reproach, and it will be given to him.

Proverbs 2:6, AMP

The Lord gives skillful and godly Wisdom; from His mouth come knowledge and understanding.

1 Corinthians 2:14, NIV

The man without the Spirit does not accept the things that come from the Spirit of God, for they are foolishness to him, and he cannot understand them, because they are spiritually discerned.

John 14:26, NKJV

"The Helper, the Holy Spirit, whom the Father will send in My name, He will teach you all things, and bring to your remembrance all things that I said to you."

Psalm 19:7, AMP

The law of the Lord is perfect, restoring the [whole] person; the testimony of the Lord is sure, making wise the simple.

1 Corinthians 2:16, NKJV

We have the mind of Christ.

136. Worth Nothing Less Than the Price He Paid

I am a chosen and redeemed person. He paid a price of unspeakable value for me. **I am worth nothing less than the price He paid.** I am bought, paid for, and covered by the precious blood of Jesus. He has made me a member of a royal priesthood, a special person belonging to the Lord. I walk in the marvelous light of His kingdom, and God grants me favor with mankind.

1 Peter 1:18, 19, AMP

You must know (recognize) that you were redeemed (ransomed) from the useless (fruitless) way of living inherited by tradition from [your] forefathers, not with corruptible things such as silver and gold, **but [you were purchased] with the precious blood of Christ** (the Messiah), like that of a [sacrificial] lamb without blemish or spot.

1 Corinthians 6:19, 20, NIV

Do you not know that your body is a temple of the Holy Spirit, who is in you, whom you have received from God? You are not your own; **you were bought at a price.** Therefore honor God with your body.

1 Peter 2:9, 10, NKJV

You are a chosen generation, a royal priesthood, a holy nation, His own special people, that you may proclaim the praises of Him who called you out of darkness into His marvelous light; who once were not a people but are now the people of God, who had not obtained mercy but now have obtained mercy.

1 John 1:7, NKJV

If we walk in the light as He is in the light, we have fellowship with one another, and the blood of Jesus Christ His Son cleanses us from all sin.

Psalm 5:12, NKJV

You, O Lord, will bless the righteous; with favor You will surround him as with a shield.

Psalm 84:11, NKJV

The Lord God is a sun and shield; the Lord will give grace and glory; no good thing will He withhold from those who walk uprightly.

137. Zealous and Burning Desire

I am always zealous for the things of God. The Holy Spirit gives me a burning desire to serve the Lord in earnest and with perseverance.

Romans 12:11, AMP

Never lag in zeal and in earnest endeavor; be aglow and burning with the Spirit, serving the Lord.

Galatians 6:9, AMP

Let us not lose heart and grow weary and faint in acting nobly and doing right, for in due time and at the appointed season we shall reap, if we do not loosen and relax our courage and faint.

Hebrews 10:36, NKJV

You have need of endurance, so that after you have done the will of God, you may receive the promise.

Exalting His Word
WITH LIFE AFFIRMATIONS FROM SCRIPTURE
Shelley Quinn

To all who long to know more of God's plan of love.
To all who want a more intimate relationship with God.
To all who look for an abundant life and power to walk in Christ's footsteps . . .
Look no further than the Bible in your hands.

Shelley Quinn knows firsthand the power and victory of not only reading the Word, but of speaking the Word—affirming promises of God aloud. In this, her previous book, *Exalting His Word,* she shares her personal story of personal healing, and how affirming God's Word became the driving force in her life.

You, too, can go beyond standing on the promises to living them out in your life.

Paperback, 176 pages.   ISBN 10: 0-8163-2147-7

3 Ways to Order:
1. Local Adventist Book Center®
2. Call 1-800-765-6955
3. Shop AdventistBookCenter.com